SMALL PETS FROM WOODS AND FIELDS

Books by Margaret Waring Buck

IN WOODS AND FIELDS

IN YARDS AND GARDENS

IN PONDS AND STREAMS

PETS FROM THE POND

SMALL PETS FROM WOODS AND FIELDS

Written and illustrated by

MARGARET WARING BUCK

11629

New York   ABINGDON PRESS   Nashville

LIBRARY
J. EUGENE SMITH LIBRARY
EASTERN CONN. STATE UNIVERSITY
WILLIMANTIC, CONN. 06226

J
502
B

Copyright © 1960 by Abingdon Press
All Rights Reserved
Printed in the United States of America
A
Library of Congress Catalog Card Number 60-5317

10-18-61

FOR DAVID

who is a friend of toads
and other creatures

Many small creatures from the woods and fields may be kept in a cage or terrarium in the home or class room. This books tells how to house and care for them.

Other creatures may be attracted to yards and gardens and enjoyed out of doors. In this book you will learn how to give them food and shelter.

The plants and animals in this book may be found in the northeastern and other parts of the United States and southern Canada.

Most of the pets mentioned here have been raised or observed by the author. In addition each section has been checked by a leading authority on the subject.

The author wishes to express thanks and appreciation to Alice Gray, Scientific Assistant, The Museum of Natural History; Professor Donald P. Rogers, Department of Botany, University of Illinois; Dorothy A. Treat, Educational Director, National Audubon Society; and Mr. John C. Orth, Assistant Superintendent, Palisades Interstate Park Commission.

LIBRARY
J. EUGENE SMITH LIBRARY
FREDERICK R. NOBLE SCHOOL
EASTERN CONN. STATE UNIVERSITY
STATE COLLEGE
WILLIMANTIC, CONN. 06226
WILLIMANTIC, CONNECTICUT

CONTENTS

PART II
INSECTS AND SPIDERS

PART III
SMALL MAMMALS AND BIRDS

PART I

PLANTS, AMPHIBIANS, AND REPTILES

TERRARIUMS

A terrarium is a container that holds earth and growing plants. Many small creatures found in woods and fields can be raised in a terrarium.

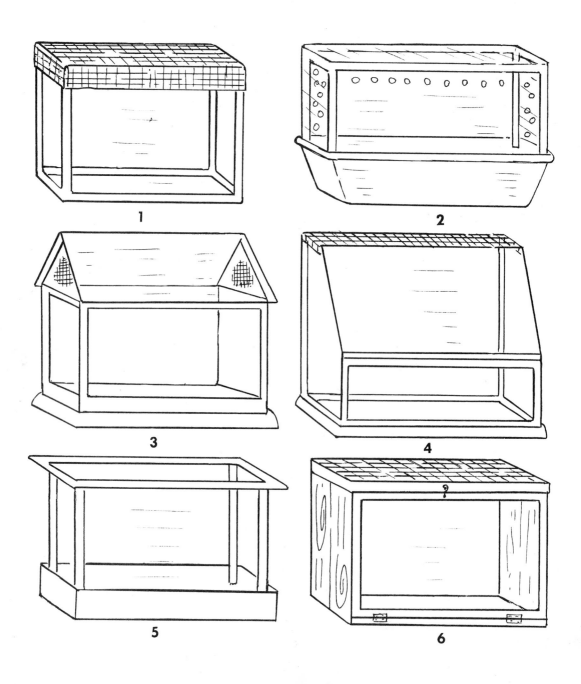

1

2

3

4

5

6

HOW TO MAKE

A terrarium is a transparent container like an aquarium. Where an aquarium has water and water plants and creatures, a terrarium has earth and land plants and creatures.

The pictures show different kinds of containers which may be used as terrariums. The terrarium may be covered by a piece of glass if it contains only plants. Thin pieces of cork or cardboard between the glass and the terrarium will provide air space. If animals are to be kept in the terrarium, it should have a piece of screen on the top or sides or enough holes to permit air to circulate.

1) A fish tank. The top is made from a rectangular piece of screen with a small square cut out of each corner and the edges bent over.

2) A window box. The top is a wooden frame covered with plastic material.

3) A miniature greenhouse. It has a wood or metal frame, glass sides and top, and a screened hole at each end near the top.

4) Another kind of greenhouse made from pieces of glass fastened together with adhesive tape. The top piece can be either screening or glass. Waterproof cement along the inside edges will make it stronger.

5) A flat pan painted to prevent rust. Four pieces of glass taped at the corners form the sides. Another piece of glass rests on top.

6) A wooden box with a glass door in front and a screen top. The wood may be given several coats of waterproof varnish, or a metal tray may be set on the bottom of the box.

7) A glass flower container with a piece of glass over the top.

8) A plastic box with holes bored in the lid.

9) A quart or gallon jar. For a top it may have a piece of mosquito netting held in place by a rubber band, or a metal screw lid with holes bored in it. It may be used upright or on the side as shown on page 12.

10) The sides are pieces of glass held together with adhesive tape. The top may be glass or screening; the bottom may be glass or varnished wood.

11) Two glass or plastic dishes, one over the other with pieces of thin cork or wood between to make an air space.

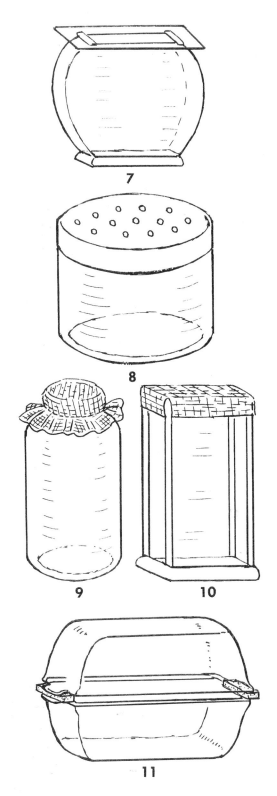

PLANTS

It is easy to grow plants in a terrarium since they seldom need to be watered. Many kinds of plants from the woods and fields will grow in terrariums.

HOW TO PLANT

Plants growing in a terrarium are pretty to look at. They also furnish shade and shelter for any small creatures that you may want to keep as terrarium pets.

In the bottom of the terrarium put a layer of coarse gravel for drainage and a few pieces of charcoal to keep the earth sweet. Then add two or three inches of earth (garden soil mixed with black dirt—leaf mold—from the woods or with peat moss) or potting soil from a garden supply store. If there are any worms or bugs in the garden soil, take them out (unless you want to leave them as food for pets) since they may eat the plant roots.

Now go out of doors and dig up some plants like the ones on the following pages. Take the plants with a ball of earth around the roots so they will not be disturbed when you move them. If the roots must be taken without earth, spread them out when you plant them. Press dirt over them so that no air pockets are left and the plants are well supported.

Some stones and fungus-covered sticks may be added for decoration. If you are going to keep animal pets, put in a dish of water also. Do not let earth or plants touch the water or they will siphon it off.

HOW TO KEEP

A desert arrangement with cacti or other plants that grow in dry places may be kept in a terrarium which is open at the top. Use a screen cover if you have pets that might crawl out. This kind of terrarium may be kept in a sunny window.

For a moist terrarium, a glass cover is necessary. This keeps the moisture from evaporating so the plants seldom need to be watered. Sprinkling with a fine spray once every week or two is usually enough. If the terrarium is tightly sealed, the plants may live for months without watering. But most plants grow better if they have a little air. To let air circulate, put thin pieces of cork or cardboard between the corners of the terrarium and the glass top.

Keep the terrarium in a window where it will get some early-morning or afternoon sun. Midday sun is too hot for most plants from woods and fields.

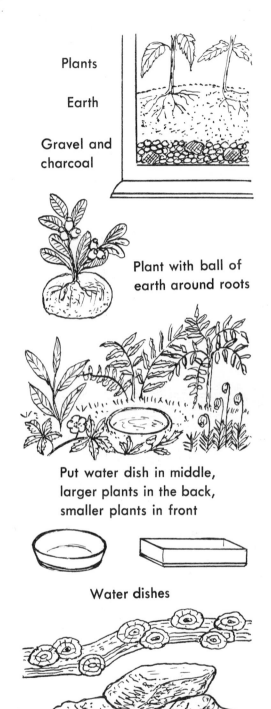

Plants

Earth

Gravel and charcoal

Plant with ball of earth around roots

Put water dish in middle, larger plants in the back, smaller plants in front

Water dishes

Stick and stones

HOW TO FURNISH

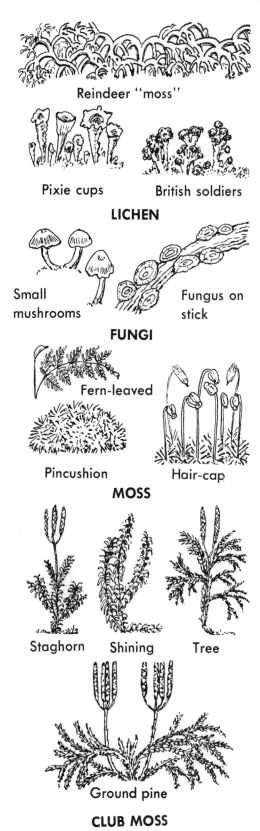

Reindeer "moss"

Pixie cups   British soldiers

LICHEN

Small mushrooms   Fungus on stick

FUNGI

Fern-leaved

Pincushion   Hair-cap

MOSS

Staghorn   Shining   Tree

Ground pine

CLUB MOSS

LICHENS

Lichens are part fungi and part algae; the latter give them a greenish color. They grow on rocks, on the bark of trees, and on patches of dry ground. REINDEER "MOSS" is a gray-green lichen with finely divided branches. It forms large tangled masses which are crisp and crunchy when dry, soft and rubbery when damp. PIXIE CUPS are gray, tinged with green or pink. The funnel-shaped cups grow to be 1 inch high. SCARLET-CRESTED CLADONIA or BRITISH SOLDIERS have grayish-green branches with scarlet tips.

FUNGI

Fungi are plants that do not have green coloring. They grow on wood, roots, and decaying material. Toadstools and other mushrooms are fungi that grow on the ground. Shelf fungi grow on the bark of trees. Collect some bright-colored fungi with pieces of what they are growing on. They will decorate the terrarium for a short time.

MOSSES AND CLUB MOSSES

Low-growing mosses may be used to carpet the bottom or to line the sides of a terrarium. FERN MOSSES have feathery leaves like tiny ferns. In moist, shady places they form large mats on the ground. PINCUSHION MOSS forms a pale green, rounded hump on roots or ground in the woods. HAIRCAP MOSSES have stems covered with needle-shaped leaves like tiny pine trees. Brown capsules bear the spores by which these mosses reproduce. The mosses grow in dry woods, in fields, or at the edge of bogs.

Club-mosses are not real mosses; they are related to the ferns. They grow on long, trailing stems which root where they touch the ground. When gathering a plant, be sure to get a root; but do not pull up enough of the stem to disturb other plants growing from it. COMMON or STAGHORN CLUB MOSS has branching stems covered with narrow, bristle-tipped leaves. SHINING CLUB MOSS has shiny leaves and spore cases that look like tiny yellow beans among the upper leaves. TREE CLUB MOSS has branches like a small spruce tree. GROUND PINE has fanlike branches. Its spore-carrying cones look like tiny candelabra.

TRAILING PLANTS AND VINES

These low-growing plants are useful because they will cover the ground and trail over stones in the terrarium.

PARTRIDGEBERRY grows in the woods. Its stems trail on the ground and send up many branches. The rounded, glossy, evergreen leaves grow in pairs along the branches. Two small white or pinkish flowers bloom at the tip of each branch in spring. Later each pair of flowers forms one red berry which may last through the winter. Sprays of partridgeberry will keep for a while in a tightly covered glass globe. A plant taken with roots and planted in a terrarium will grow for a long time.

TWINFLOWER also has a trailing stem with short branches. Its evergreen leaves are scalloped and somewhat rough and leathery. In summer it has pairs of small, nodding, bell-shaped flowers that are white outside and pinkish or purple and hairy inside. This plant is found in cool woods in either moist or dry places.

Partridgeberry and twinflower will grow in a moist terrarium which is shaded from hot sunlight.

YELLOW TREFOIL or BLACK MEDIC is a small clover with trailing stems which grows in waste places. The tiny flowers are yellow, and the seeds are black. The three-parted leaves are bluish-green.

GROUND IVY or GILL-OVER-THE-GROUND grows along roadsides and in fields and lawns where there is some shade and moisture. Its scalloped, heart-shaped leaves grow in pairs along a trailing stem. In the early spring it has small purple flowers.

COMMON CINQUEFOIL or FIVE-FINGER is a weed that grows in dry fields and waste places. Tufts of leaves rise from its trailing stem. The leaves are smooth, sharply toothed, and divided into five parts. There are small yellow flowers in spring and summer.

Clover and five-finger will grow in a fairly dry and sunny terrarium.

MONEYWORT or CREEPING CHARLIE grows in moist meadows and sometimes in lawns. It has a long trailing stem with paired, shining, bright green leaves. In spring and summer it has yellow flowers.

Ground ivy and moneywort will grow in a moist terrarium in a partly sunny place.

PARTRIDGEBERRY

TWINFLOWER

BLACK MEDIC

GILL-OVER-THE-GROUND

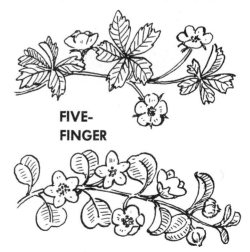

FIVE-FINGER

CREEPING CHARLIE

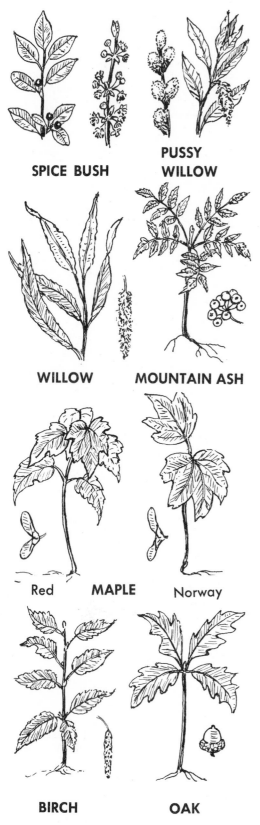

SPICE BUSH   PUSSY WILLOW

WILLOW   MOUNTAIN ASH

Red   MAPLE   Norway

BIRCH   OAK

SHRUBS AND TREES

Tiny shrubs and trees that have just started to grow from seeds (seedlings) are good terrarium plants. They furnish shelter for pets and give them something to climb on. You will find seedlings growing under or near large trees and shrubs. If seedlings are not available, you can take a small leafy branch and stick it in the earth in the terrarium. It will stay green for a while and may form roots. Seeds can also be planted, but some kinds take a long time to start growing.

In spring or summer a flowering twig from any kind of a shrub that has small flowers may be used. The SPICE BUSH, with its clusters of tiny yellow flowers which blossom before the leaves appear, is good. In fall use a twig with berries like the thorny, red-fruited BARBERRY.

A twig from a PUSSY WILLOW shrub will grow if it is kept in water or planted in moist earth. Twigs may be cut when they have the fuzzy catkins in spring or when they have their long narrow leaves in summer.

Twigs from willow trees take root easily if they are kept moist. Willow leaves are long and narrow. They grow on long branches which droop in the WEEPING WILLOW and are upright in the BLACK WILLOW and other kinds.

MOUNTAIN ASH seedlings make fine terrarium plants. Their long leaves, which are divided into many leaflets, look like ferns. The seedlings develop from orange berries which grow in clusters on the trees and drop to the ground in late fall. Put some of the berry clusters in the terrarium for a spot of color; later some of them may grow.

A seedling from any kind of a maple tree may be used. The RED MAPLE which you will find in moist places is one of the finest. It has a red-brown stem and rather narrow leaves which are green, tinged with red. The NORWAY MAPLE, which you see along village streets, has larger, wide, green leaves that are cut into five lobes.

A seedling from any kind of BIRCH TREE—paper, gray, yellow, or black—makes a pretty terrarium plant. The elliptical or triangular leaves have saw-toothed edges. The flowers and seeds are in catkins.

Plant an acorn or an OAK seedling at the back or side of the terrarium. Oak leaves are cut into deep lobes and are dark green, sometimes tinged with red.

EVERGREENS

Tiny evergreen trees and shrubs are especially good to grow in a terrarium. If you can't find seedlings, take small twigs and stick them in the earth. They will look like little trees and will stay green for a while. Cones may be used, also. They are decorative and a source of food for seed-eating creatures.

Dwarf BLUEBERRY bushes complete with berries are sometimes found growing in a blueberry patch. The bushes have woody stems and long, leathery, evergreen leaves. In spring they have clusters of tiny white or pinkish flowers which are followed by the dark blue berries. The little bushes will grow in a dry, sunny terrarium.

BAYBERRY shrubs grow in sandy places. They have rather narrow, glossy, evergreen leaves. In spring there are catkins along the twigs; in summer there are green berries which later turn bluish-gray. In fall use a small twig of bayberry to decorate the terrarium.

A spray of HEMLOCK or a seedling makes a graceful addition to a terrarium. Hemlock branches are more flexible than those of most evergreens. The short needles are dark green on top, light underneath. They grow in flat rows along the twigs. Mature trees have small brown cones that hang from the tips of the twigs.

PINE trees have long needles that grow in clusters along the stems. A seedling has one or more clusters, like upturned tassels, on its single stem. Large pine trees have brown cones. Pine and hemlock seedlings like a moist, shaded terrarium.

SPRUCE trees have short, sharp needles that grow close together around the stems. Their stiff branches spread out like fans or fingers. Mature trees have short, rounded, light brown cones. You will find spruce trees in cool woods, often on dry hillsides.

CEDAR or JUNIPER trees grow in dry meadows and on stony hillsides. Mature trees have fan-shaped branches with scalelike leaves, and berries that are first green, then gray, then blue in late summer and fall. Young cedar trees have bristly, sharp needles at first and scalelike leaves later.

Cedar and spruce seedlings will grow well in a rather dry, sunny terrarium.

BLUEBERRY   BAYBERRY

HEMLOCK

WHITE PINE

RED SPRUCE

RED CEDAR

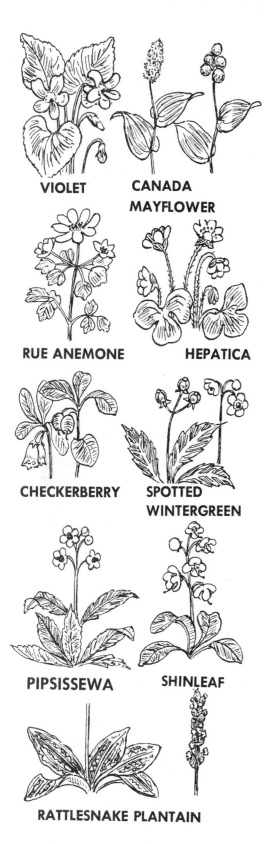

VIOLET CANADA MAYFLOWER

RUE ANEMONE HEPATICA

CHECKERBERRY SPOTTED WINTERGREEN

PIPSISSEWA SHINLEAF

RATTLESNAKE PLANTAIN

WOODLAND PLANTS

In the woods you will find many small plants that will grow well in a shaded terrarium. With the owner's permission you may dig up a few of them; take some woods soil for them to grow in.

VIOLETS are pretty in spring. Some kinds grow at the edge of the woods; other kinds grow in damp or dry meadows. Look for the tiny, sweet-smelling, white violet and the smaller varieties of purple violets.

Large patches of CANADA MAYFLOWER may be found in rocky woods. The plants have heart-shaped leaves and angular stems which grow to be 6 inches high. In spring they have clusters of dainty white flowers, and in autumn they have red berries.

RUE ANEMONE is a delicate plant with three-lobed leaves and white flowers in early spring. It grows to be about 6 inches high. The WOOD ANEMONE is a slightly larger plant with divided leaves and a single white flower.

The HEPATICA is one of the first flowers to bloom in spring. It has purple, blue, or white flowers on hairy stems 3 or 4 inches high. Its three-lobed leaves live through the winter and may be red-brown in spring.

WINTERGREEN or CHECKERBERRY has a cluster of evergreen leaves at the top of a woody stem that grows to be about 6 inches high. In summer a pair of small, bell-shaped flowers nod under the leaves. The red berries which come in fall and the leaves have the wintergreen flavor.

SPOTTED WINTERGREEN has dark evergreen leaves that have white streaks and toothed edges. Its reddish-brown stem grows to be 9 inches high. In summer it has a cluster of waxlike, creamy-white or pink flowers.

PRINCE'S PINE or PIPSISSEWA grows to be 12 inches high. It has groups of shining, evergreen leaves along its green or brownish stem. A cluster of fragrant, white flowers appears at the top of the stem in summer.

The rounded, evergreen leaves of the SHINLEAF grow in a cluster near the ground. In early summer fragrant, waxy, white flowers bloom on a stem 5 to 10 inches high.

The bluish-green, white-veined leaves of the RATTLE-SNAKE PLANTAIN grow in a whorl close to the ground. The leaves last through winter. In summer it has a stem 6 to 12 inches high with a spiral of tiny white flowers.

FERNS

Ferns thrive in the atmosphere of a moist terrarium. They grow best in rich earth from the woods and in a place away from strong sunlight. Small terrarium pets, like salamanders and frogs, use ferns to hide under.

The LADY FERN has lacy leaves that grow to be 2 feet tall and often bend over at the tips. Their smooth stalks rise in clusters from a creeping rootstalk. This fern is found in meadows, woods, and along stone walls.

WOOD FERNS have lacy leaves; in some kinds they are evergreen. The leaf stalks have brown scales. They grow in clusters from 1 to 3 feet tall. You will find these ferns in rich mountain woods, in swamps, and in rocky places.

The EBONY SPLEENWORT has narrow, dark green leaves on shiny, ebony-brown stalks. Several graceful leaf stalks rise from a thick, spiky root. This fern grows in woods, fields, or on banks in moist, rocky soil.

The MAIDENHAIR FERN also has a smooth, shiny, dark brown stalk. Small fan-shaped leaflets form a large leaf which is circular or horseshoe-shaped. This is one of the most beautiful of our ferns. It grows in rich, rocky soil in the woods.

The CHRISTMAS FERN is so named because it is green at Christmas time as well as in summer. Its dark green, wavy leaflets grow along a scaly stalk. The young, rolled-up leaves, which appear in spring, are grayish and furry. Young plants grow well in a terrarium in soil taken from the woods and mixed with sand.

The ROCK FERN looks much like a small Christmas fern. It has flat leaflets on a smooth stalk. It grows on rocks in fields and along streams. Plant it on a stone in the terrarium.

The ROYAL FERN has narrow, pale green leaflets, widely spaced on the stem. The stalks are smooth and sometimes reddish. In summer it has clusters of beadlike spore cases at the top of the stem. This fern grows to be 5 feet high and is found in moist woodlands, in swamps, or along ponds and streams.

The SENSITIVE FERN has wavy leaflets and a wide vein down the center stem. The spores are in beadlike cases in rows at the top of a separate stem. This fern grows in sun or shade, in moist or dry places at the edge of woods.

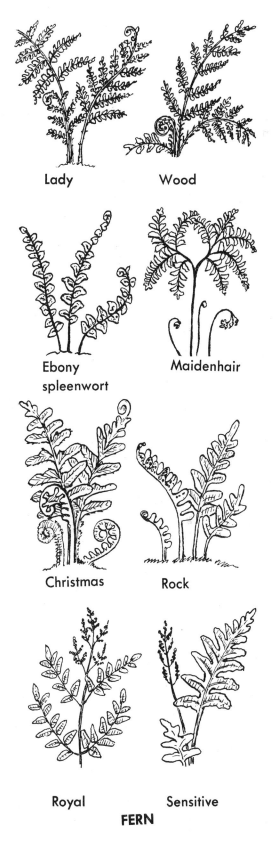

Lady

Wood

Ebony spleenwort

Maidenhair

Christmas

Rock

Royal

Sensitive

FERN

AMPHIBIANS

Amphibians are creatures that live both on land and in the water. They like the moist atmosphere of a terrarium with plants and a dish of water.

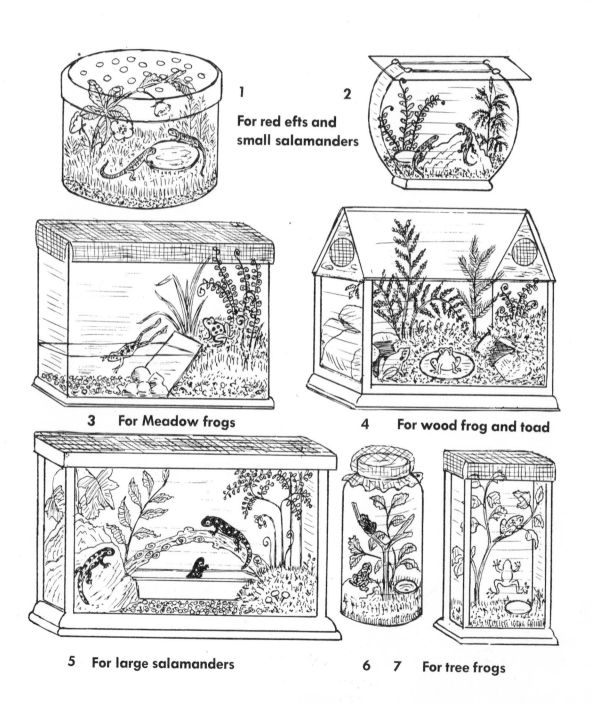

1

2

For red efts and small salamanders

3   For Meadow frogs

4   For wood frog and toad

5   For large salamanders

6   7   For tree frogs

Frogs, toads, and salamanders are amphibians. Most of them spend the first part, or larval stage of their lives in water. When they become adults, some live on land, some in water, and some both on land and in water.

HOW TO KEEP

For amphibians a moist and airy terrarium is needed. Keep it in a place where it will not receive direct sunlight, since sun shining on glass creates too much heat.

Some kinds of terrariums to use for amphibians are shown on the opposite page. 1) A plastic box. Holes are bored in the lid with a hot wire or nail. 2) A glass jar or vase. The top is a piece of glass set on slices of cork to provide an air space. 3) A glass tank for creatures that like an equal amount of land and water. The land and water areas are separated by a piece of glass which is as wide as the tank and is held in place by stones. 4) A miniature greenhouse with grass, moss, and ferns growing in it, stones, and a saucer of water. Air enters through screened holes near the top. 5) A large terrarium with a pan of water, a stick bridge, stones, and plants. Its top is a piece of screen tacked to a wood frame. 6) and 7) Tall glass containers for creatures that like to climb. Each has grass or moss on the bottom, dry branches, growing trees or vines, and a small container of water. The top covering is a piece of mosquito netting held in place by a rubber band or string, or a piece of wire screen.

The top covering of the terrarium should fit securely, since most amphibians can climb up the glass sides and slither out through a small opening. A piece of wire window screening may be fastened to a wood frame that fits the terrarium top. Or screening may be used without a frame if a piece is cut a little larger than the top of the terrarium. A square is cut out of each corner, and the sides are bent down. For a small terrarium, a lid with holes punched in it, mosquito netting, or cheesecloth, or a piece of glass set on slices of cork may be used.

The terrarium should be furnished to resemble the place where the creature in it lived when it was out of doors. Moss, ferns, and other plants, sticks, stones, and a container of water, will make a woodsy home.

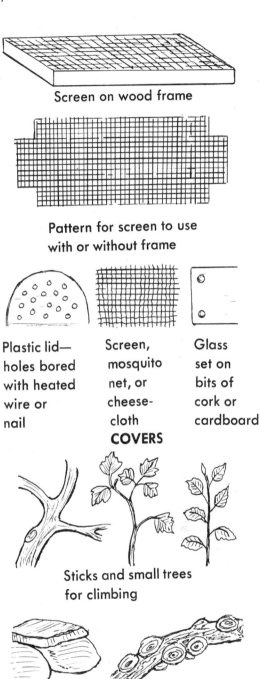

Screen on wood frame

Pattern for screen to use with or without frame

Plastic lid— holes bored with heated wire or nail

Screen, mosquito net, or cheese- cloth

Glass set on bits of cork or cardboard

COVERS

Sticks and small trees for climbing

Stones for den

Stick for bridge

Dishes for water

FURNISHINGS

LIBRARY
FREDERICK R. NOBLE SCHOOL
STATE TEACHERS COLLEGE
WILLIMANTIC, CONNECTICUT

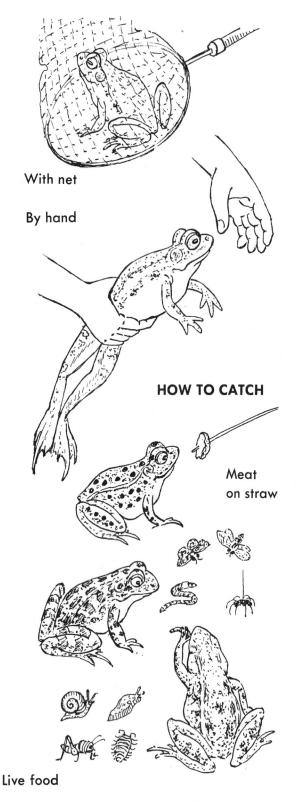

With net

By hand

HOW TO CATCH

Meat
on straw

Live food

HOW TO FEED

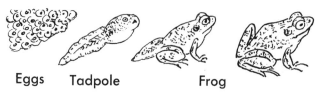

Eggs   Tadpole   Frog

LIFE HISTORY

Frogs and toads lay eggs in masses or strings of jelly in fresh water. The eggs hatch into tadpoles which later change into frogs or toads. Some frogs live in water, other frogs and toads live on land. In winter, out of doors, they hibernate. Indoors they do not hibernate, but they are not very active.

HOW TO CATCH AND CARRY

You can catch frogs and toads with a small-meshed net or with your hand. If you can get close to a frog, try moving one hand in front of it to catch its attention, then grab its hind legs with the other hand. At night you can dazzle a frog with a flashlight while you grab it.

Carry frogs and toads home in a cloth or mesh bag (one to a bag), a covered box (with air holes), or a covered basket.

HOW TO FEED

Wild frogs and toads eat insects, worms, grubs, pill bugs, snails, and slugs. Frogs also eat fish, tadpoles, and smaller frogs. In addition to their natural food, captive frogs and toads will eat pieces of raw beef, liver, and fish. Put a piece on the end of a toothpick or broom straw and wave it in front of your pets.

A frog or a toad pushes large pieces of food into its mouth with its front feet and closes its eyes when it swallows. Its tongue is fastened to the front of its lower jaw. To catch insects it shoots its tongue out. Catch some house flies or collect fruit flies for your pets and watch the fun that follows.

Frogs and toads should be fed every day or two in summer, although they can go without food for a longer time if necessary. In winter they should be offered food every few days even though they may not eat.

TREE FROGS

There are several kinds of native tree frogs. They all live on land, in trees, in shrubs, or in the grass. (In spring they enter ponds to mate and lay their eggs.) Sticky pads on their toes enable them to cling to branches and to climb the glass sides of a terrarium. Keep them in a terrarium large enough to give them space to climb or jump about; a wide-mouthed gallon jar or a tall, straight-sided glass container will work well. Put moss or grass on the bottom and place a dish of water on it. Have some growing vines, tiny trees, or branches for the frogs to climb.

CRICKET FROGS live among the weeds that border swamps and ponds. They cannot climb trees but they can leap high. The spring mating call of the male, made with the throat distended, is a clicking sound like a cricket's chirp. These frogs grow to be about an inch long. They are brown, grayish, or olive-green, and have dark spots on the back with a green line down the middle.

SPRING PEEPERS live in meadows and woods. They can be found among fallen leaves on the ground or in bushes and trees. They are light or dark brown and have a dark cross on the back, colors which blend with their natural surroundings. Full-grown peepers are only an inch long. In early spring you can hear them peeping in ponds and pools. With a flashlight in the evening you may be able to see them and possibly to catch a pair for your terrarium. In summer tiny peepers that were recently tadpoles are easier to catch but harder to find. In the terrarium peepers need only a shallow container of water, like the top of a jar, since they can flatten out and soak in a few drops of water.

The TREE FROG or TREE TOAD is larger than the other frogs on this page. It grows to be 2 inches long. Its back is gray, grayish-green, or brownish-gray, and has an irregular dark blotch. Underneath, it is whitish with orange under the hind legs. Large pads on its toes permit it to climb trees. It leaps about like a tiny acrobat, and can even hang from a branch with one foot. One, or better two, tree frogs make friendly and contented pets in a terrarium where they have room to move around. They feed in late afternoon and evening. The male frog makes a trilling sound with his throat distended.

Male's throat swells when he chirps

CRICKET FROG

Peeper bathes in a few drops of water

SPRING PEEPER

Tree frogs are acrobats

Male frog makes a trilling sound

TREE FROG

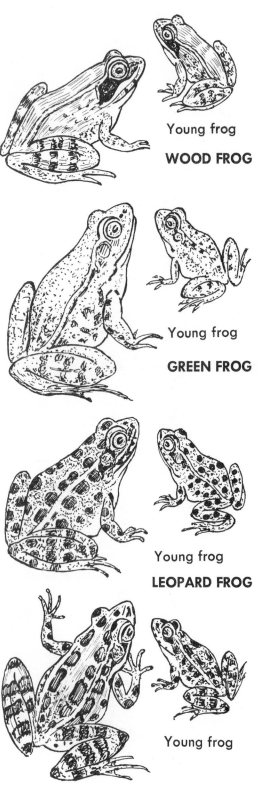

Young frog
WOOD FROG

Young frog
GREEN FROG

Young frog
LEOPARD FROG

Young frog
PICKEREL FROG

WOOD FROG

This frog lives on the ground in the woods most of the time. In early spring it enters a pond to mate and lay eggs. In summer its tadpoles change into ½ -inch frogs. When one year old, the frogs are an inch long; at four years, they are full grown, about 2½ inches long. They are light or dark brown and have a black patch behind the eye.

Wood frogs may be kept in a terrarium that has a dish of water, moss and ferns, and a little stone house. (A wood frog and a toad were kept together in a terrarium where each had its own stone house to which it retired.)

MEADOW FROGS

These frogs live in or near water most of the time. In summer they may be found in meadows. Small frogs, about an inch long, may be found near the edge of a pond. These are the best size to catch for pets. It will be a year or more before they become too large for the average terrarium. (Then they should be set free near a pond.) Meadow frogs may be kept in a terrarium that has land and water areas.

GREEN FROGS have green or brownish backs with some dark markings, bright green heads, and shoulders, and white underparts with some black spots along the sides. A light-colored fold of skin runs along each side. The breeding male has a yellow throat. Young frogs are olive-brown or greenish and have black specks on their backs, and bright green specks on their cheeks. Green frogs grow to be 4 inches long. The female is larger than the male.

LEOPARD FROGS have green or brownish backs with rounded black spots which are outlined in white. Underneath, the frogs are white. The males grow to be about 3 inches long and the females about 4 inches. The upper-sides of newly formed frogs are green with black polka dots. Alert and friendly, these frogs make delightful pets.

The upper sides of PICKEREL FROGS are a greenish brown. The dark spots on their backs are somewhat rectangular. Underneath, the frogs are white with some orange under the hind legs. The young frogs are slender and shy; they do not make as good pets as leopard frogs.

TOADS

Toads live on the ground except in the breeding season.

AMERICAN TOADS (the common, garden variety) are brown with dark spots and light markings. Underneath they are light with some black spots. The male grows to be 3½ inches, the female to be over 5 inches long. They have a dry, warty skin which they shed several times a year. If they are annoyed, glands under the skin may give off a fluid which is poisonous if it gets into the eyes or mouth of another animal. It will not cause warts.

Young toads, newly changed from tadpoles, are less than ½ inch long. They are olive or light brown and have dark brown spots. Early in summer you may be able to find some of them along the bank of a pond. Two or three in a terrarium make amusing pets. Feed them twice a day. They will eat aphids, fruit flies, and other small insects, and tiny worms. As they grow larger, they will learn to take bits of raw meat from a straw. Soon the little toads will be as broad as they are long. In spite of their shape, they are agile and can climb up the sides of a terrarium. Sometimes they like to spread out and soak in a shallow dish of water. Larger toads like to burrow into soft earth or hide under stones or leaves.

FOWLER'S TOADS are found in fields and gardens, as are the American toads, but they are usually not so common. Their backs are yellowish or greenish-gray and have dark spots and also a yellow stripe down the middle; underneath they are white. The male grows to be 2 inches long, the female, 3 inches. They go to ponds to breed late in the spring.

SPADEFOOT TOADS live on damp, loose earth or on sandy soil. In rainy weather during spring and summer, they enter ponds to breed. This toad has a short, compact body which grows to be 2⅞ inches long. Its back is dark brown and is streaked with yellow bands. Underneath it is white. Its bulging eyes have vertical pupils. Spadefoot toads are not often seen, although they are common in some places, because they burrow under loose soil in the daytime and are most active at night.

Keep spadefoot toads in a terrarium with loose, damp earth or sand. It is interesting to watch them dig, but they are too retiring to make good pets.

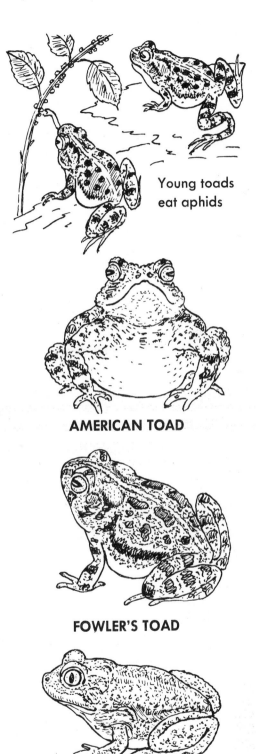

Young toads eat aphids

AMERICAN TOAD

FOWLER'S TOAD

SPADEFOOT TOAD

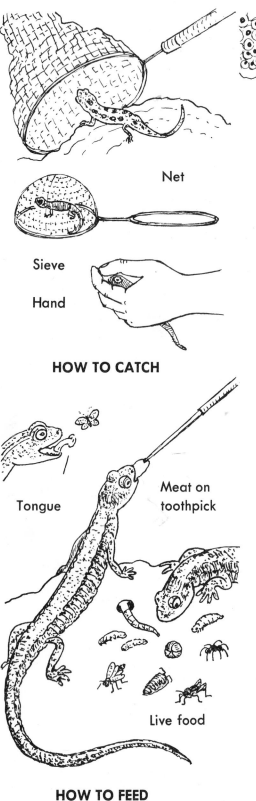

Net

Sieve

Hand

HOW TO CATCH

Tongue

Meat on toothpick

Live food

HOW TO FEED

Eggs

Larva

SALAMANDERS: LIFE HISTORY

Some salamanders go to ponds in spring to mate and lay eggs, and some lay their eggs in damp places on the ground. The jelly-coated eggs hatch into larvae, most of which have outside gills and live in water. A few grow up on land. Most of the larvae change into salamanders in summer.

HOW TO CATCH AND CARRY

Catch salamanders with a net, sieve or scoop, or by hand. Salamanders are slippery and often slimy, but they are not poisonous to touch. Do not grab them by their tails, because the tails of some kinds break off easily.

Carry captured salamanders in a covered box or can with holes punched in the lid for air. Do not crowd them or let them become overheated. Some moist moss or grass in the bottom of the container makes a good mattress.

HOW TO FEED

Small salamanders eat small earthworms, white worms, insects, bits of raw meat and liver, and raw fish. In addition, large salamanders eat millipedes, pill bugs, spiders, snails, caterpillars, crickets, and other small creatures.

When feeding meat or fish to salamanders, put the food on the end of a broomstraw, on a toothpick stuck into a grass or weed stem, or on a string, or hold it with forceps or tweezers. Wave it in front of the salamander. If it is hungry, it will creep up to the meat or fish, bite it, and pull it off with a jerk of its head.

Many salamanders are active only at night. These you can feed in the evening, or you can leave live food, such as earthworms, in the terrarium for them to eat at any time. Salamanders can go without food for some time if necessary, but it is best to feed them two or three times a week. In winter they are less active and eat very little.

LUNGLESS SALAMANDERS

These slender, medium-sized salamanders do not have lungs; they breathe through a throat membrane and through their skin, which must be kept moist. They avoid sunlight and are most active at night or in rainy weather. They make good pets, although they may hide during the day. Keep them in a terrarium that has moss and other growing plants, and a dish of water. The ground should be sprinkled often enough to keep it moist, and the terrarium should be shaded from hot sun. Cover the terrarium securely, because salamanders can crawl up glass.

The DUSKY SALAMANDER lives along springs and rocky streams. It grows to be 4½ inches long. The larvae are brown with two rows of light spots on the back. Young adults are reddish- or grayish-brown and have dark specks on the back; old adults are all dark brown. Both have a light line from eye to mouth.

In summer the female lays clusters of jelly-coated eggs on damp land under stones, leaves, or other covering. She usually guards them for about two months until they hatch. The newly-hatched larvae soon develop tail fins and gills. Then they crawl to the nearest water.

The SLIMY SALAMANDER has glands in its skin that give off a fluid that sticks to your hands if you touch it. This salamander is shiny black and has small silvery spots on its back. It grows to be about 7 inches long. It lives on land, even in the larval stage, usually in rocky woods. The female lays eggs in clusters under rocks or in other sheltered places, probably in winter or early spring. When the young hatch, they are about ½ inch long.

The RED-BACKED SALAMANDER also lives all of its life on land, usually in the woods. It is found in places that would be too dry for most salamanders. However, if the weather is unusually dry, it will burrow into the ground and stay there until it rains. In spring or summer the female salamander lays clusters of eggs in logs, under stones, or in other sheltered places. The young are 1 inch long when they hatch. They are well developed, since they have passed most of the larval stage in the egg. The adults are slender and grow to be 3 to 5 inches long. They have two color phases: some are all dark gray or brown; others are gray on the sides and brick red on the back.

Female guards eggs

DUSKY SALAMANDER

SLIMY SALAMANDER

Gray color

Red color

RED-BACKED SALAMANDER

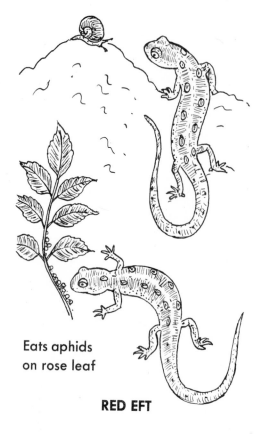

Eats aphids
on rose leaf

RED EFT

RED EFT

The eft is the land form of the spotted newt, a salamander which lives in water. The female newt lays eggs, usually in spring, in a pond or lake. The eggs hatch into larvae which live in water until the end of summer. Then the larvae change into efts. Their gills are replaced by lungs, their tail fin disappears, and their color changes from green to red. Their backs are brownish-red or orange-red and have red spots; underneath they are orange or yellow, and they have black spots on the sides. They grow to be 2 inches long. During autumn they roam among fallen leaves and rocks in the woods; in winter they hibernate under stones or logs, or in other shelters. The following spring, or a year or two later, they go to ponds and change into olive-green and yellow newts. In some places the eft stage is skipped; in other places, including terrariums, the eft may remain as such for several years. Efts are good pets to keep in a covered terrarium. Put some moss and other plants from the woods on the bottom, also a shallow dish of water. Feed the efts aphids and other small insects, pieces of earthworm, and bits of raw meat from the end of a straw.

MOLE SALAMANDERS

These large, stout-bodied, broad-headed salamanders live on moist land or in the woods, but at breeding time they go to ponds to lay their eggs. They breathe air through lungs. Although some of these salamanders may live in your neighborhood, you may not see them, because they are most active at night. You may happen to find one by overturning a stone or a log in moist woods.

Keep mole salamanders in a large terrarium that is moist and shaded from the sun. On the bottom have several inches of loose earth, some woodland plants, a few pieces of bark, and a large dish of water. These salamanders may hide all day and come out at night to feed.

JEFFERSON'S SALAMANDER grows to be 7 inches or longer. Older individuals are dark brown or gray all over; younger ones have light blue spots on the sides and back. All have longer toes than most salamanders. Early in spring they enter ponds to lay their eggs.

Hides under leaves,
stones, or logs

JEFFERSON'S SALAMANDER

The MARBLED SALAMANDER lives in sandy, rocky places. Its back is dark gray or black and has white bars. Underneath, it is bluish. It grows to be about 5 inches long. These salamanders breed in autumn. The female lays her eggs near a pond or swamp on the ground, in little depressions under bark, moss, logs, or other shelter. She stays with the eggs, her body helping to keep them moist, until they are flooded by late rains. The eggs hatch in late winter or spring, usually in a rainy season. The larvae wriggle to the water and live in it until the following summer. Then they change into adult salamanders.

The SPOTTED SALAMANDER has a shiny black back with large, round, yellow spots; underneath, it is gray with light blue specks. It grows to be over 7 inches long. In early spring large numbers of spotted salamanders may collect in ponds to breed. The females lay their eggs in jelly-coated masses in the water. You may not see these salamanders unless you are out with a flashlight at night, but you may find their egg masses in the morning. Most of the year these salamanders live in damp places in woods and meadows, in gardens, or even in damp cellars. Although they may hide during the day, spotted salamanders make interesting terrarium pets. They have been known to live for twenty-four years.

The TIGER SALAMANDER is black with yellowish blotches on the back, is yellow under the chin, and is gray underneath the body. The females grow to be about 7 inches long and the males 8 inches. Early in spring they enter ponds to breed and to lay masses of eggs in the water. The eggs hatch into larvae which live in water until the end of summer. Then they lose their gills and change into air-breathing salamanders which live on land. In some parts of the Southwestern United States the adult salamanders retain their gills and remain water creatures all their lives. In this form they are known as axolotls or, sometimes, "water dogs." Axolotls can reproduce and may continue as water-living creatures for many generations.

Larvae and axolotls should be kept in an aquarium. Adult tiger salamanders may be kept in a large terrarium where they make hardy and odd-looking pets. These salamanders are found throughout the United States. They are rare in the East, abundant in the West and Southwest.

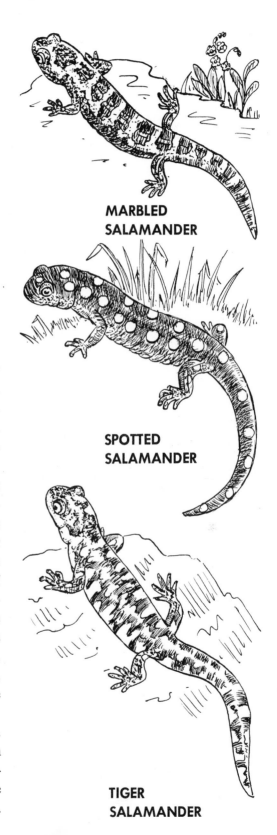

MARBLED
SALAMANDER

SPOTTED
SALAMANDER

TIGER
SALAMANDER

REPTILES

Reptiles are cold-blooded, usually scaly, creatures that live on land. Many small reptiles will live in a rather dry terrarium with screen top.

Miniature greenhouse
for Carolina anole

Desert terrarium for
horned lizards

FOR LIZARDS

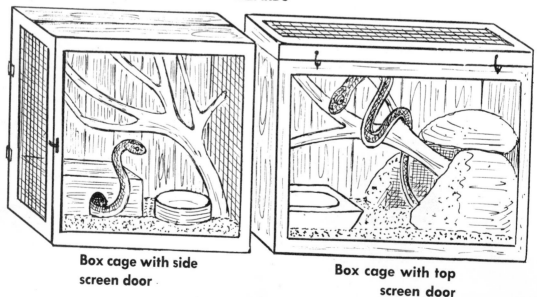

Box cage with side
screen door

Box cage with top
screen door

FOR SNAKES

HOW TO KEEP

Most reptiles like a warm, dry, sunny place. They may be kept in a terrarium or cage with glass or wood sides and a screen top or side. Try to place the terrarium or cage so that the sun will shine through the screen instead of the glass. Sun on glass is likely to be too hot. Also have some shelter in the form of growing plants, a pile of stones, pieces of bark, or an overturned box with a hole in the side. Plants should be sprinkled once in a while to keep them from drying out. This will also furnish drinking water for some kinds of reptiles.

A dish of water should be provided for bathing. The dish should be large enough to allow the reptile to sit in it and submerge. (A snake will curl up in the dish.)

LIZARDS, except the anole, like dry places. Their terrarium should have sand or loose earth on the bottom and some rocks, sticks, and growing vines or other plants. To make a desert terrarium for a horned lizard, put several inches of sand on the bottom, purchase some small cactus plants in pots and sink the pots into the sand.

TURTLES like a terrarium that resembles the woods where they live. Put earth in the bottom, and then plant moss, ferns, grass, or other plants. Water-living turtles should have enough water to swim in; land-living turtles need just enough water for bathing. Large turtles may be kept in a yard in a fenced enclosure in which they will have some shade at all times. (Too much sun may be fatal.) If no one objects, they may also be allowed to roam in a house. They should not be confined in a small space.

SNAKES will live in a wooden box with a screen top or screen side and a glass front. If the box is given a coat of waterproof varnish, it will be easier to keep clean. The glass front, side screen, or screen top can be made into a door with hinges on one side and a lock on the other. Be sure the screen is firmly fastened to the box and the door locked so the snake cannot push its way out.

On the bottom of the box have a tray of sand that can be removed for cleaning or a layer of pebbles that can be replaced, a dish of water for bathing, a forked stick for climbing, a piece of rough bark to rub against while the skin is being shed, and a rocky cave or a box with a hole in the side for hiding in.

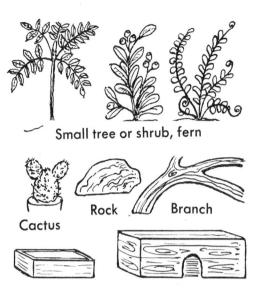

Small tree or shrub, fern

Cactus   Rock   Branch

FURNISHINGS

Woodland terrarium

FOR SKINKS

Terrariums with ferns and water dish

FOR TURTLES

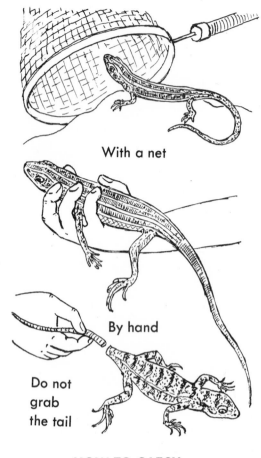

With a net

By hand

Do not
grab
the tail

HOW TO CATCH

Eggs

Young

LIFE HISTORY

LIZARDS

Lizards look something like salamanders; but they are reptiles, not amphibians. They have dry, scaly skins, and claws on their feet. They live on land at all stages of their life. They like sun and are active during the day.

Most kinds of lizards lay eggs. The eggs are oval with leathery or papery shells. Look for eggs in rotting stumps or under logs or leaves. To raise the eggs, put them in a container with moss on the bottom and cover them with sand or sawdust. Keep them moist but not wet. At room temperature they will hatch in a few weeks.

HOW TO CATCH AND CARRY

Lizards are not easy to catch, because they move swiftly. If you find one basking in the sun, you may be able to get a net over it or possibly catch it with your hand. Do not grab a lizard by the tail or you may be left with a wriggling tail in your hand while the rest of the animal darts away.

Carry a captured lizard in a covered box with holes in the lid or in a covered basket. Do not put large and small lizards together.

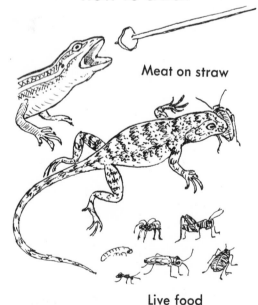

Meat on straw

Live food

HOW TO FEED

HOW TO FEED

The lizards on these pages catch insects with a flick of the tongue and eat them. Small lizards eat ants, flies, moths, small bugs, and beetles. Large lizards eat spiders, beetles, grasshoppers, crickets, and other large insects and their grubs; they also eat small animals including smaller lizards. Most lizards will eat meal worms, but they do not like earthworms. Some kinds will learn to take raw meat from the end of a straw and some will lap up raw egg yolk.

Lizards can go for a long time without food, but it is best to feed them two or three times a week.

CAROLINA ANOLE

The Carolina anole, or American chameleon, is a slender, delicate lizard which grows to be about 6 inches long. It is light green or brown on the back and white underneath. The male has a reddish-orange pouch under his throat. He expands his pouch and nods his head either to attract a mate or to warn a rival male. When two males meet, they may fight, each one trying to bite off the other's tail. If one succeeds, he walks off with the still-wriggling tail in his mouth.

The anole changes its color as a result of fear, change of light, temperature, or surroundings. It may be cinnamon brown when on dark earth and bright green when on a green leaf. Several times a year an anole sheds its skin.

On each foot the anole has five long toes which have claws and sticky pads underneath. It is able to climb and to cling to trees and walls. It often makes acrobatic leaps while chasing insects. When it sleeps, it stretches out along a branch or drapes itself over a leaf. It can close it eyes, and it can also turn them without moving its head.

In the Southeastern states the anole is found on trees and bushes in wild places and also in gardens and greenhouses. In other parts of the country it is often sold in pet shops or at fairs because it makes an unusual and interesting pet. Keep one anole or more in a tall terrarium with moss or grass on the bottom and with growing vines (ivy is good) or small trees for the anole to climb on. It is necessary to sprinkle the plants frequently because the anole sips drops of water instead of drinking from a dish.

Make a little pile of stones in the terrarium to furnish shelter. An anole likes sun, but there should be shelter available in case it becomes too hot.

A wild anole eats insects which it catches by creeping up on them and swiftly thrusting out its sticky tongue. In captivity it will eat many insects including: flies, small grasshoppers, crickets, cockroaches, moths, grubs, and spiders. It will not take earthworms; but it will eat mealworms (which you can get from a pet store), although it cannot live on them alone. It cannot live on sugar-water either. In winter in the northern states it is a difficult pet to feed. If you have an anole which will not eat, give it to a zoo if you can get to one.

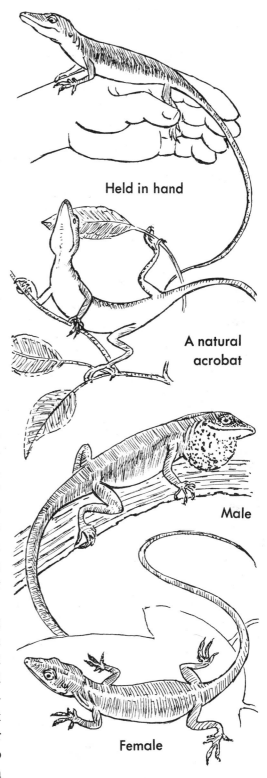

Held in hand

A natural acrobat

Male

Female

CAROLINA ANOLE

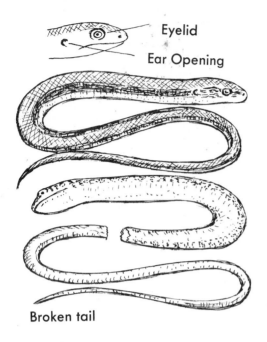

Eyelid

Ear Opening

Broken tail

GLASS SNAKE LIZARD

Female guards eggs

Old male

BLUE-TAILED SKINK

GLASS SNAKE LIZARD

The glass snake is another southern species that may be kept as a pet because of its oddity. Although it is without legs and looks like a snake, it is a lizard. It has eyelids, ear openings, a scaly underside, and a replaceable tail, which a snake does not have. This lizard has a shiny, glassy appearance. Its back is black, olive, or brown and has small green spots on each scale; underneath, it is greenish-white. It grows to be 3 feet long, about ⅔ of which is its tail. The tail is brittle and breaks off easily. Some people think that a glass snake can break in two and grow together again. This is not true, but the body of the snake can live after the tail is lost. The tail is replaced by a shorter one.

The glass snake eats earthworms, slugs, insects, and other small animal life. It often burrows underground. Keep it in a screened terrarium that has several inches of earth and some growing plants on the bottom.

BLUE-TAILED SKINK

Blue-tailed or five-lined skinks are covered with small, smooth, shiny scales. Young skinks are black or dark brown and have five white or yellow stripes running down the back and sides; underneath they are light; and their tails are bright blue. As they grow older, their body color becomes lighter, their stripes darker, and their tails gray. Old males are olive-brown with broad-cheeked reddish heads. This skink grows to be 7½ inches long. It is found among rocks, fallen leaves, or bark in the woods. Although it is more common in the South, it is also found in southern New England. The GREATER FIVE-LINED SKINK, sometimes called a "scorpion" in the southern states, grows to be 10 inches long. It usually lives in trees.

Keep skinks in a large screened terrarium with stones, moss, and growing vines or small trees, and a shallow dish of water. Captive skinks will eat many kinds of insects and their grubs; some will take bits of raw meat or lap up a little raw egg. Like a snake, a skink may open its mouth to "taste" the air. Larger skinks will eat smaller ones, so do not keep different sizes together. A large male may bite if handled, but its bite is not deep or poisonous. In winter, even in a warm terrarium, skinks sleep most of the time.

FENCE LIZARD OR SWIFT

This lizard grows to be about 7 inches long. It has rough scales on its body and has long toes and a thin tail. It is brown or gray on the back, white underneath. The female has dark, wavy bars on her back; the male has blue patches on his sides and a black patch under his chin. The female lays thin-shelled oval eggs about ½ inch long.

Fence lizards are found in the eastern states. They live in dry woods, especially pine woods. In damp, cool weather they hide in stumps or wood piles. In sunny weather they run about or sit on fences or other convenient spots to sun themselves. If they see someone coming, they may keep still at first and then take off like a flash. You will not find them easy to catch. If you are able to capture one or two, keep them in a dry terrarium in a sunny place. Put several inches of sand on the bottom of the terrarium; then add some pieces of rotted wood, bark, and flat stones for the lizards to hide under. Feed them live insects including beetles and grubs, cockroaches, or meal worms.

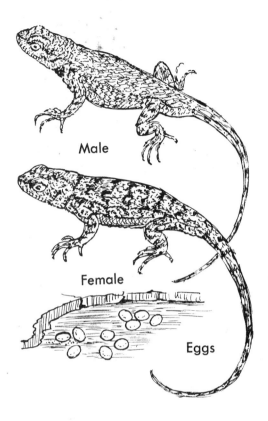

Male

Female

Eggs

FENCE LIZARD

HORNED LIZARD OR HORNED TOAD

Several kinds of horned lizards live in the southwestern states. They are often kept as pets and are sometimes sold in pet shops. A horned lizard has a wide, flat body from 3 to 7 inches long and a short tail. Its back is gray or brownish and has darker spots and sometimes a light line down the middle; underneath, it is light colored. It has horns on its head and rows of spines along its sides. It can close its eyes and can spurt blood from an extra eyelid which breaks when it gets excited. It may also puff up or play dead if it is alarmed. Unlike other lizards, it may be picked up by its tail, which does not break off. Some kinds of horned lizards lay eggs. Other kinds bear their young alive.

Keep horned lizards in a dry container such as the desert terrarium on page 30. Put the terrarium in a warm, sunny place. Give the lizards a shallow dish of water for bathing and a leaf of lettuce or other plant with drops of water on it for drinking. Feed them insects and grubs. The lizard's favorite food is ants. You can collect ants on a piece of paper by putting honey or jam on it and leaving it beside an ant hill for a short time.

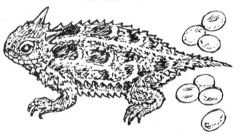

Some kinds lay eggs

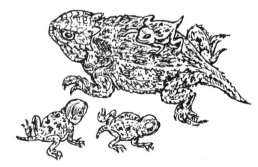

Some bear young alive

HORNED LIZARDS

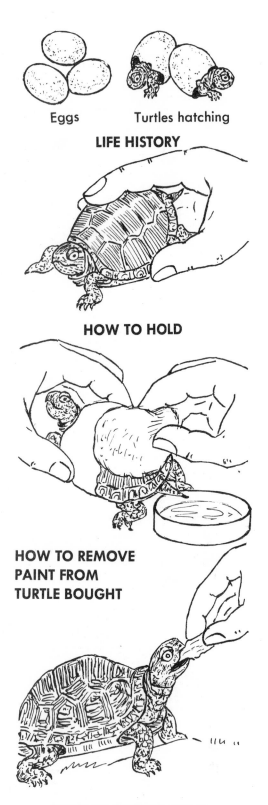

Eggs **Turtles hatching**

LIFE HISTORY

HOW TO HOLD

HOW TO REMOVE PAINT FROM TURTLE BOUGHT

HOW TO FEED BY HAND

TURTLES: LIFE HISTORY

Female turtles lay eggs which hatch into baby turtles.

If you find some turtle eggs, you might try hatching two or three at home. Keep them in a container with sand in the bottom and cover them with loose moss or cotton. They should be kept moist but not wet. Once in a while you can take an egg out and hold it up to the light to see the young turtle developing inside. It will hatch in two or three months. It takes a turtle four years or longer to mature. After that, it may live for twenty-five years or longer.

HOW TO CATCH AND CARRY

Only small turtles are suitable for a terrarium. On land you can pick them up with your hand. Hold a turtle by the middle edge of the upper shell so it can't scratch or bite you. Be careful not to drop it, because a cracked shell can be fatal. You can catch a swimming turtle with a fish net.

Carry the turtle home in a covered box (with air holes) or a covered basket.

If you buy a turtle instead of finding one, and it has a painted shell, you should remove the paint as soon as possible. Dip a wad of cotton in turpentine, kerosene, or nail polish remover and rub the paint until it is soft enough to rub or scrape off. Protect the turtle's head from the fumes while you are working.

HOW TO FEED

Turtles eat both animal and vegetable food. They tear the food apart with their horny jaws (they do not have teeth) and with the claws of their front feet. Water turtles eat under water; land turtles eat on the ground.

For living animal food, give turtles: insects, grubs, snails, and earthworms. For more animal food give them bits of raw beef, liver, chicken, or fish. About once a week add a few drops of cod-liver oil and a pinch of bone meal.

For vegetable food give turtles: growing plants in the terrarium, berries, bananas, carrots, spinach, lettuce and other greens, and wild mushrooms.

Feed baby turtles every day. Older turtles should be fed about three times a week.

KINDS OF TURTLES

Young turtles that live on land are the best kind to keep in a terrarium. Small pond turtles may be kept in a terrarium that has a large container of water.

The two land turtles of the northeastern states are the box turtle and the wood turtle. They both make good pets, but in some states permission to keep them must be obtained from the State Department of Conservation.

BOX TURTLE

The upper shell, or carapace, of the box turtle is high and arched; it is black or dark brown in color and has yellow spots and streaks. This turtle grows to be about 5 inches long. The under shell, or plastron, is yellow and brown. It is hinged near the middle and can be drawn tightly against the upper shell, completely boxing in the turtle's body. The male turtle has red eyes and the female has brown or yellow eyes.

With her hind legs the female digs a hole in soft soil in a field early in summer and lays three to eight eggs. The eggs have thin, flexible, white shells a little over an inch long. In about three months the eggs hatch into small turtles which are able to take care of themselves.

In winter box turtles hibernate underground. In summer they roam in woods and fields; sometimes one will enter a pond to cool off or to escape from an enemy.

WOOD TURTLE

This turtle grows to be 7 inches long. Its upper shell is flatter than that of the box turtle and is brown with yellow and black markings. It has lines and ridges that give it a sculptured look. (If you find a turtle whose shell looks dry and dusty, you can polish it with vegetable oil.) The undersides of the turtle's neck, tail, and legs are brick red. The male has longer claws and a longer tail than the female.

In June the female turtle lays two to twelve white, papery-shelled eggs in a hole in a sandy place. At the end of summer the eggs hatch into small turtles with almost-round shells and long tails.

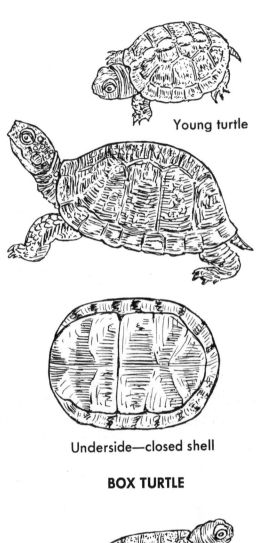

Young turtle

Underside—closed shell

BOX TURTLE

Young turtle

WOOD TURTLE

Eggs   Young born alive

LIFE HISTORY

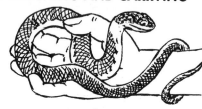

Nooses

Forked stick

Collecting bag

FOR CATCHING AND CARRYING

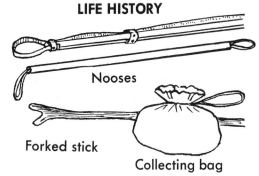

HOW TO HOLD A SMALL TAME SNAKE

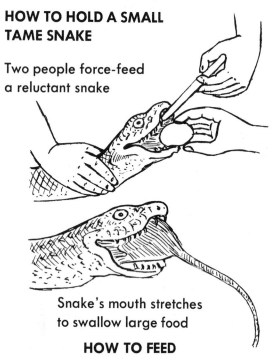

Two people force-feed a reluctant snake

Snake's mouth stretches to swallow large food

HOW TO FEED

SNAKES

Snakes are reptiles that do not have any feet. Some kinds of snakes bear their young alive, other kinds lay eggs.

HOW TO CATCH AND CARRY

To catch a snake you will need a 3-foot-long stick with a forked end or a stick with a noose at one end. If the snake's head is near the ground, pin it down with the forked stick. If its head is raised, slip the noose over it and pull the string at the other end of the stick to tighten the noose. With one hand grasp the snake around the neck firmly but do not squeeze it. With the other hand hold the snake in the middle. Ease the snake into the collecting bag which is open on the ground. Or slide the bag over the snake while it is pinned to the ground. The collecting bag should be made of canvas or other stout cloth and should have a drawstring.

HOW TO FEED

A snake's jaws are held together with ligaments that stretch to let the mouth open wide and take in food wider than the snake's head. The skin of the body can stretch, too. The snake's under jaw has two parts which can be moved one at a time to pull food into the mouth.

Most snakes will eat insects such as crickets, grasshoppers, cockroaches, smooth caterpillers and grubs; earthworms; salamanders; lizards; eggs; tadpoles and frogs. Some snakes will eat small fishes. Large snakes will eat small animals including mice and rats. They usually should be dead when put into the cage; if alive they may injure the snake. Some snakes will learn to eat raw meat or fish from the end of a string, straw, tweezers, or fingers. If captive snakes refuse to eat, they may be force-fed a few times before they are set free. While one person holds the snake's neck and keeps its mouth open with a blunt knife, the other person inserts a piece of food.

If small food is given, feed the snake every day or two. If larger food is given and eaten, the snake may not need food again for a week or longer. In winter a snake may not eat much, but it is best to offer it food occasionally.

SNAKES AS PETS

Poisonous snakes should not be kept as pets. The ones on these pages are not poisonous. You may keep small snakes for a while in a terrarium or cage in order to watch and study them. You will see that snakes cannot close their eyes, that they cannot hear but do sense vibrations, that they flick their tongues in and out to "taste" the air or sense their surroundings, and that they shed their skins once in a while as they grow.

Some snakes become tame, are willing to be handled, and learn to take food from the fingers. Others will not eat in captivity; these should be set free after they have been observed for a while.

A snake flicks its tongue to taste the air

LIVE-BEARING SNAKES

The female GARTER SNAKE bears from twelve to seventy young snakes.

Garter snakes usually have a light yellow stripe down the middle of the back and a dark brown stripe on each side; underneath they are white. They vary somewhat in color. They grow to be 3 feet long. You will find garter snakes in gardens, fields and woods, and near water where they catch and eat minnows. When captured, they may bite and give off a bad odor; but they lose these bad habits when they become tame.

Captive garter snakes will eat earthworms, pieces of raw fish, and other foods.

The RIBBON SNAKE is more slender and brightly marked than the garter snake. It has three yellow and two brown stripes along the back and sides, and is white underneath. The female bears about twelve young ones which are 8 or 9 inches long. Ribbon snakes will eat small frogs and pieces of raw fish. They may be too nervous to make good pets.

The DE KAY'S or BROWN SNAKE is found in fields and yards. It grows to be a foot long or a little longer. Its back, which is brown, has a lighter stripe down the middle and rows of checkered dark brown spots along each side; underneath, it is pinkish. The young are darker colored and are about 4 inches long when they are born in August. In captivity De Kay's snakes are gentle; they will eat earthworms and grubs.

Young snakes

GARTER SNAKE

RIBBON SNAKE

DeKAY'S or BROWN SNAKE

Eggs

GREEN SNAKE

Young

RING-NECKED SNAKE

MILK SNAKE

Young hatching

BLACK SNAKE

EGG-LAYING SNAKES

Snake eggs are likely to be found in a hollow log, under a rock, or in the ground. They are either capsule-shaped or rounded, and are leathery, light colored, and an inch or more long. In the northeastern and some of the central states the egg-laying snakes are harmless. If you want to hatch a few eggs at home, keep them in a warm place in a container with wood pulp, moss, or loose earth. See that they remain moist but not wet. The eggs become rounder and larger as the young snakes develop inside. Eggs laid in early summer hatch by late summer or fall.

Most young snakes will eat insects, grubs, and earthworms. As a young snake grows, it sheds its skin frequently. It may double its length in the first year.

The SMOOTH GREEN SNAKE is leaf green above and pale green or white underneath. It lives in grassy fields and grows to be 20 inches long. As a pet it is pretty and gentle; it does not bite or try to escape if handled.

A growing plant in a pot set in the green snake's cage will give it something to climb on. Feed the snake crickets, grasshoppers, smooth caterpillars and other insects, and spiders. It will eat three or four crickets a day.

The RING-NECKED SNAKE is a slender snake that grows to be about a foot long. Its back is glossy gray; underneath, it is bright orange with dark spots along the sides. It has a yellow ring around its neck. It lives in wild places, but is sometimes found in vacant lots and parks. During the day it hides under leaves, logs, or stones; at night it comes out to feed. It eats earthworms, insects, small toads, and salamanders. This snake makes a gentle pet although it may give off a musky odor if disturbed.

The MILK SNAKE is found around barns. Its back is gray with patches of brown or red bordered by black, and it grows to be about 3 feet long. It eats mice and rats. Although it makes a gentle pet, it may not feed well.

BLACK SNAKES grow to be 6 feet long. They are bluish-black on the back and gray underneath. They have white throats and chins. Newly hatched snakes are about 8 inches long. Until they are two or three years old, the young snakes are gray marked with black-edged reddish blotches, much like a milk snake. Black snakes eat insects; frogs; mice, rats and other small animals; and birds' eggs.

PART II

INSECTS AND SPIDERS

VIVARIUMS

A vivarium is a container for live creatures. You can make them for insects and spiders from the transparent containers found around the house.

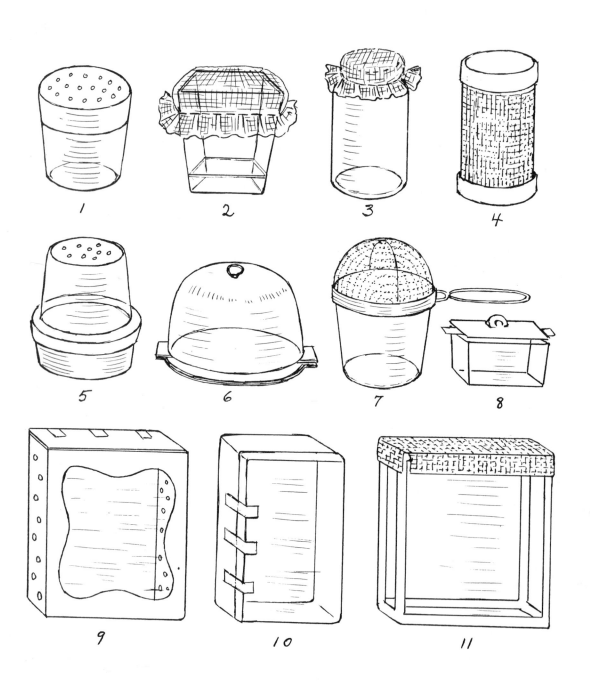

HOW TO MAKE

Almost any kind of a transparent container may be used for keeping insects. A piece of netting over the top or holes punched in the lid or sides will allow air to enter. (Holes may be made in a plastic container with a heated wire or nail.)

On page 42 are pictures of vivariums made from containers that may be found in most households.

1) A round plastic box with holes in its cover.

2) A plastic refrigerator box with a square piece of netting over the top and held in place with a rubber band.

3) A quart jar with a wide mouth and a round piece of netting fastened over the top with a rubber band.

4) A roll of wire screening with top and bottom rounds cut from a cereal container.

5) A shallow flower pot or round pan holds earth for growing plants. An upside-down plastic container is the cover.

6) A cake plate with a plastic cover. Pieces of cardboard between plate and cover allow air to enter.

7) A squat glass jar with a kitchen strainer over it.

8) A covered glass butter dish with slightly raised lid.

9) A cardboard cake box with a plastic window. Holes are punched in the sides. The top has adhesive tape hinges so it can be opened.

10) A cardboard box with holes punched in the sides. A plastic lid is fastened on one side with tape hinges to make a door.

11) A box made from five pieces of glass fastened together with adhesive tape. A piece of wire screening bent over the sides forms a removable lid.

Some kinds of insects need growing plants, cut flowers, or twigs in their vivariums. To keep cut flowers and leaves fresh, put them in a bottle of water. Use a bottle with a small mouth or one with a lid that has a hole bored in it. If the water isn't covered, the insect may fall in and drown. Dry twigs may be set in a can filled with pebbles or a flower pot filled with sand.

Plants or twigs in a container may be enclosed with a glass lamp chimney or a tube made from a roll of transparent plastic material. Cover the top of the chimney or tube with a piece of cheesecloth or mosquito netting.

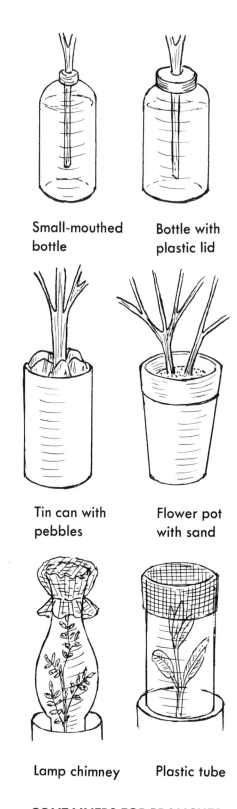

Small-mouthed bottle

Bottle with plastic lid

Tin can with pebbles

Flower pot with sand

Lamp chimney

Plastic tube

CONTAINERS FOR BRANCHES

INSECTS AND SPIDERS

In a vivarium you can watch an insect or spider's life cycle. You can admire its beauty and see how it changes in appearance and habits as it grows.

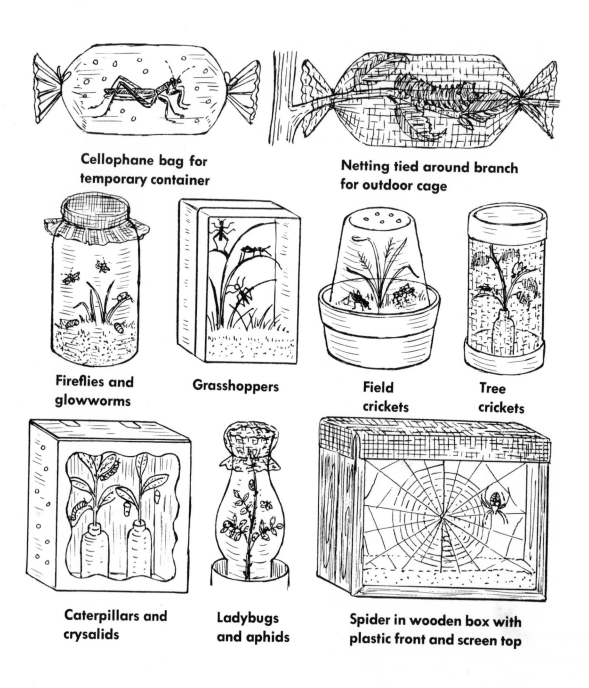

Cellophane bag for temporary container

Netting tied around branch for outdoor cage

Fireflies and glowworms

Grasshoppers

Field crickets

Tree crickets

Caterpillars and crysalids

Ladybugs and aphids

Spider in wooden box with plastic front and screen top

Insects and spiders make good summer pets. They do not require much space, and they are easy to find and feed.

You will find insects almost everywhere: in flowers; on the leaves of plants and trees; under bark, logs and stones; in underground burrows; and sometimes in the house.

HOW TO CATCH

A lightweight net can be made with a coat hanger and a piece of cheesecloth, mosquito netting, or net curtain material. Pull the coat hanger into a circle to make the rim. Straighten out the handle of the coat hanger and fasten it with wire, tape, or staples to a pole or stick that is about 3 feet long.

Sew the netting to the rim with button and carpet thread and bind it with tape to make it stronger. The net should be long enough to fold over so that captured insects can be kept inside. This kind of net is useful for catching small flying insects. The kind of butterfly net one buys is stronger and better for catching large flying insects.

A heavy net for sweeping through grass and bushes may be made of muslin or other strong cotton material fastened to a strong wire rim. Attach the rim to a short pole.

To collect insects from a bush or tree, place an open umbrella underneath and beat the branches with a stick.

A sieve may be used to sift through fallen leaves and dirt. Dig up insects in the ground, find them under stones, or pry them from loose bark with a knife or trowel.

To catch insects found on a flat surface, slip a drinking glass or jar over them, then slide a thin piece of cardboard under the glass or jar.

To catch beetles, tape half a pill box to your thumb and the other half to your other fingers. Snap the box together and catch the beetle inside. Ground beetles may be caught in a tin can, an olive bottle, or a fruit jar baited with molasses or meat. Sink the can or jar up to its neck in the ground. A board or stone above it will keep out the rain.

At night insects will be attracted by street lights or lighted windows, or can be found with a flashlight.

Captured insects may be picked up in a piece of cloth, on a spoon, with forceps or tweezers, or if they do not bite, with fingers.

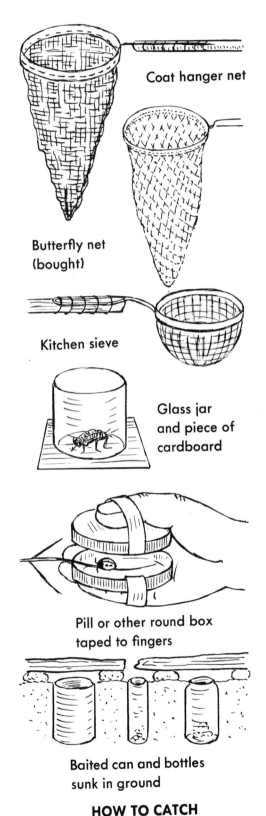

Coat hanger net

Butterfly net (bought)

Kitchen sieve

Glass jar and piece of cardboard

Pill or other round box taped to fingers

Baited can and bottles sunk in ground

HOW TO CATCH

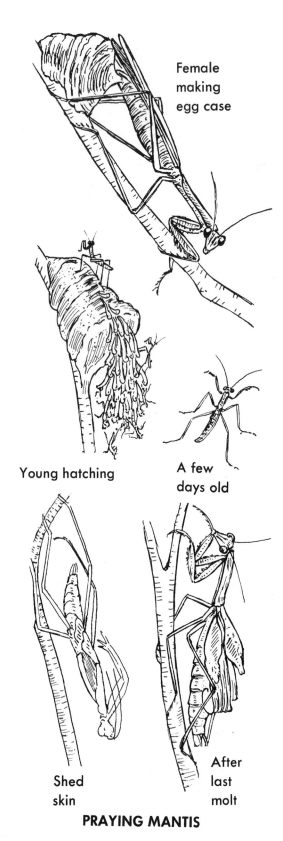

Female making egg case

Young hatching

A few days old

Shed skin

After last molt

PRAYING MANTIS

PRAYING MANTIS: LIFE HISTORY

One of the most interesting and easily kept insect pets is the praying mantis. It has a brown or green body, and green, or brown and green wings. Some kinds grow to be 2 inches long, others grow to be 4 inches long. In early autumn the female mantis makes an egg case on a weed stalk or a branch of a tree or bush. Clinging upside down, she discharges a froth from her tail end and lays her eggs inside of it. The froth hardens into a case in which the eggs live through the winter. Shown in the picture is the mantis which originally came from China and is now common in the northeastern states.

WHERE TO FIND AND HOW TO CATCH

Look for mantises among weeds in fields or vacant lots. You can pick one up easily since it moves slowly. It will not bite, but it may cling to your hand with its spiny feet. Pull it off gently so as not to injure its slender legs. Put it into a shoe box to carry home. If you find an egg case, collect it with a piece of the stem to which it is fastened.

HOW TO KEEP

Through the winter keep the egg case in a cool place in a container covered with a piece of mosquito netting. Late in spring the young mantises will pour out of the side of the case, about two hundred of them, each the size of a large mosquito. Set most of them free outside in a field or garden. Put a few into a vivarium. As they grow, they will shed their skins and their wings will grow longer.

HOW TO FEED

Young mantises will eat aphids (tiny insects often found on rose bushes and other plants) and fruit flies. If they do not get enough of these, they will eat each other. Large mantises will eat: flies, moths, grasshoppers, crickets, and other insects; also meal worms and spiders. They will learn to eat bits of raw meat from the end of a straw.

They drink water from a spoon or from drops on leaves. After eating, the mantis cleans its face and feet.

ANTS

Ants live in colonies underground. Each colony has a queen (an oversized ant) and worker ants. The queen lays eggs which hatch into grubs. The grubs form cocoons and change into worker ants. The workers dig tunnels, find food, clean up, raise the young, and perform other duties.

To watch ants at work, you can dig up a colony and put it into a glass house. To construct an ant house, make a frame from four pieces of wood, each about ½ inch wide. Fasten a piece of glass to the front and back of the frame with adhesive tape. Make holes in the top so you can put in food and water. Keep corks or cotton in the holes when not in use. Instead of using glass, you can cover the frame with a tough plastic film. Before fastening the top piece of the frame, fill the house ¾ full of dirt and put in the ants.

A wide, flat bottle with a cork or a fine net over the top may also be used for an ant house. Or you could try a plastic box with feeding holes punched in the top.

Keep the ant house in the dark or put a piece of cardboard over it when you are not watching it.

Feed the ants two or three times a week with a few drops of honey or molasses, tiny bits of raw meat, nuts, apples, bananas, or dead insects. See which kind of food your colony likes best. Some kinds of ants eat some foods, others eat other foods. Add a few drops of water once a week or keep a moist sponge in the ant house.

ANT LION

In a sheltered, dry spot, sometimes under a porch, you may find a little hole, or pit, with sloping sides. This is the home of the ant lion, a small grub with a flat body and large, pincer-shaped jaws. It lives at the bottom of the pit. There it lies in wait and catches ants and other insects that fall in.

To see how the ant lion makes its pit and catches its food, dig one up and put it in a shallow bowl filled with sand. After the pit is made, put some ants or other small insects on the sand at the edge of the pit.

When the ant lion is full grown, it makes a round silken cocoon in the sand. After a few weeks inside the cocoon, it sheds its skin and emerges as a winged insect.

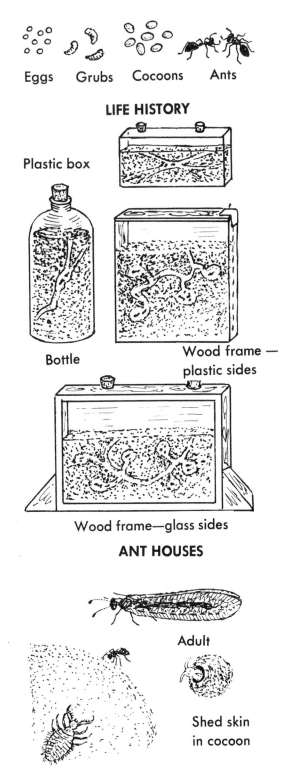

Eggs Grubs Cocoons Ants

LIFE HISTORY

Plastic box

Bottle

Wood frame — plastic sides

Wood frame—glass sides

ANT HOUSES

Adult

Shed skin in cocoon

ANT LION or DOODLEBUG

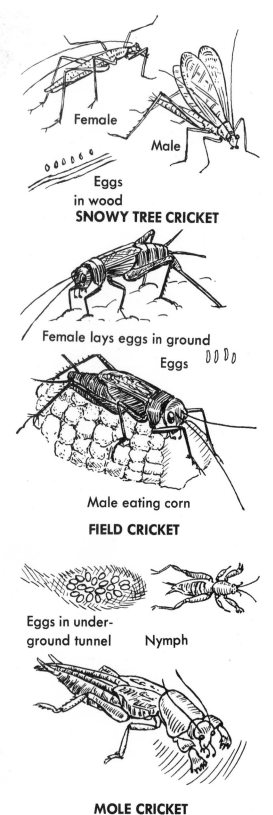

Female

Male

Eggs
in wood
SNOWY TREE CRICKET

Female lays eggs in ground

Eggs

Male eating corn

FIELD CRICKET

Eggs in under-
ground tunnel   Nymph

MOLE CRICKET

CRICKETS

There are several different kinds of crickets. They lay eggs either in the ground or in trees or shrubs. The eggs hatch into wingless nymphs. The nymphs grow and molt until wings form and they are adult crickets.

As pets, crickets are musical as well as entertaining.

SNOWY TREE CRICKETS are less than an inch long, and are pale green. The male has gauzy wings. If you can catch a male, you may be able to see how he chirps. He raises his wings and rubs them rapidly against each other. Tree crickets chirp at night in unison; the hotter the night, the faster they make their repeated "waa" sound.

Look for tree crickets on the leaves of trees and bushes. Keep them in a vivarium and give them leaves, fruit, aphids, and other tiny insects to eat.

Black FIELD CRICKETS grow to be about an inch long. They live on the ground under rocks or other shelters. They may be found in yards, gardens, lots, and fields. In the fall they often get into houses. The male chirps both day and night by rubbing one wing over the other. One that was kept in a vivarium chirped loudly until he was given a female companion, then his chirps became softer. The male cricket has larger wings than the female. She has short wings and a long spear at the end of her body through which she lays her eggs in the ground.

Do not keep large and small crickets together. Large crickets may eat the small ones. If two male crickets are kept together, they may fight. The Chinese sometimes keep fighting crickets as a sport, like fighting cocks.

Feed field crickets raw vegetables, fruit, dog biscuits, crackers, moist bread, and bone meal or a little raw meat. Young crickets eat roots and small insects.

The MOLE CRICKET is about ½ inch longer than the field cricket. It is brownish on the back and lighter underneath. It has large front feet with which it digs underground tunnels, like a mole. If you can find one of these crickets, put it into a container with some damp earth. Then you can see how it digs its tunnel.

Look for mole crickets in damp ground. They may appear at the mouth of their tunnels at night when they are most active. They make a churring sound when they chirp. These crickets eat roots, earthworms and grubs.

GRASSHOPPERS

There are long- and short-horned grasshoppers. The long-horned kind are musical; the short-horned kind are acrobatic.

The Katydid is one kind of long-horned grasshopper. It grows to be about 2 inches long and has wings that look like leaves. To sing, it rubs one wing over the other. The TRUE KATYDID, which is named after its song, has rounded wings. The BUSH KATYDID, which makes a sharp "tzeet, tzeet" sound, has long wings that taper to a point.

Katydids lay their eggs on the leaves or bark of trees and bushes.

Because they look so much like the leaves they live among, katydids are not easy to see. You may happen to discover one in a bush or tree. Or you may find one when it is singing at night by shining a flashlight on it.

A captive katydid may be fed leaves from trees and shrubs, lettuce leaves, and fruit.

SHORT-HORNED GRASSHOPPERS or LOCUSTS live among the weeds in fields and vacant lots. Some kinds sing, or fiddle, by rubbing their rough hind legs over their wings. Others rattle their hind wings against their front ones while flying. Most of these grasshoppers lay their eggs in the ground.

Locusts zig-zag about when you approach, but you can usually catch a few with an insect net, a glass jar, or your hands. Put them in a fairly large vivarium, and they will continue their antics. You can imagine that they are circus performers.

A few inches of earth on the bottom of the vivarium will give the locusts a place to lay their eggs. Plant some grass and keep it moist so that it will grow and furnish food. For more food add pieces of fruit and vegetables.

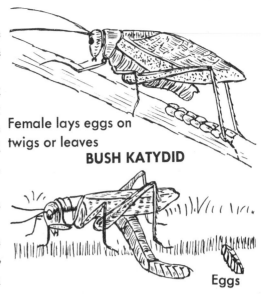

Female lays eggs on twigs or leaves

BUSH KATYDID

GRASSHOPPER

Female lays eggs in ground

Eggs

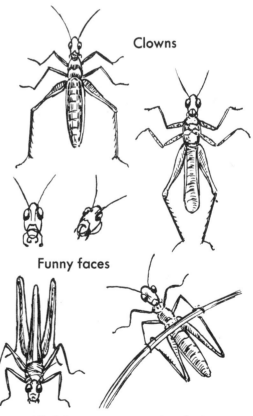

Clowns

Funny faces

Tight-rope walker

High jumper   Acrobat

GRASSHOPPER CIRCUS

BUTTERFLY CATERPILLARS

It is fun to raise caterpillars and watch them change into beautiful butterflies.

LIFE HISTORY

Female butterflies lay eggs on leaves. These leaves are always the kind that the caterpillar that hatches from the eggs likes to eat. Caterpillars are smooth or spiny, and striped, mottled, or spotted. Full-grown caterpillars are less than ½ inch long to over 2 inches long. When they are full grown, they form chrysalises. From the chrysalis the butterfly emerges. It hangs from the chrysalis until its crumpled wings have stretched and it can fly away.

HOW TO KEEP

Keep caterpillars on a branch of the plant on which you find them. Set the branch in a bottle of water. Choose a bottle with a small neck, or if you must use a wide-mouthed bottle, put the branch through a lid with a hole in the middle. If an open bottle is used, the caterpillar may fall in and drown. When the caterpillar forms its chrysalis, it will hang from a stem or leaf or from the top or sides of the container. After the butterfly emerges, it is best to set it free as soon as its wings have hardened. Then it can find flowers from which to sip the nectar that is its food.

MONARCH BUTTERFLY

This butterfly lays pale green eggs on the underside of milkweed leaves. The eggs hatch into tiny caterpillars which eat the milkweed leaves. The caterpillars grow and shed their skins several times. They have white, black, and yellow bands on their bodies, and two black horns at both the head and tail end. When they are about twelve days old, they hang themselves up by their tail end. The next day the caterpillar skin splits, and the chrysalis which has formed inside wriggles out. It has a jade green case with a band of gold beads near the top. After seven to ten days the dark colors of the butterfly's wings begin to show through the case. Soon the orange and black monarch butterfly emerges.

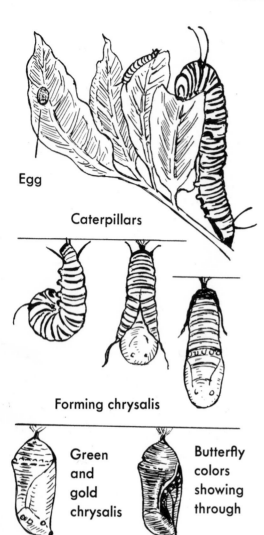

Egg

Caterpillars

Forming chrysalis

Green and gold chrysalis

Butterfly colors showing through

Butterfly coming out of chrysalis

MONARCH BUTTERFLY

PAINTED BEAUTY AND PAINTED LADY

The caterpillar that turns into the PAINTED BEAUTY is spiny and has a black body with white lines and spots. You will find it on white everlasting plants in fields in summer. While the caterpillar is small, it lives in a nest made from the down of the leaves or from the flower petals. When it is full grown, about 1½ inches long, the caterpillar fastens its tail end to some support and hangs there while it forms a gray chrysalis. If it is late in the season, the butterfly may not come out until the following spring; but usually it comes in about ten days.

The upper wings of the painted beauty butterfly are golden brown with black markings and white spots. The under wings have a beautiful lacy pattern of white lines on brown. There are two dark eyespots on the hind wings.

The PAINTED LADY butterfly is much like the painted beauty in color, but the lady has a row of small eyespots on the hind wings instead of two large ones. Its caterpillars are spiny and have black bodies with yellow markings. They live on thistle plants, where they make nests.

BLACK SWALLOWTAIL

The caterpillar of this butterfly is found on parsley, Queen Anne's lace, and other plants of the parsley family. When young, it has a spiny black body with yellow spots and a band of white through the middle. As it grows larger, it becomes smooth and green with black bands and yellow spots. If it is annoyed, it thrusts out two orange horns which give off a bad odor. When the caterpillar is grown and is nearly 2 inches long, it fastens itself to a support by silk threads at the tail end and around the middle of the body. Then it forms a greenish or brown chrysalis. About ten days later a beautiful swallowtail butterfly emerges. It is black with yellow and blue spots on its wings.

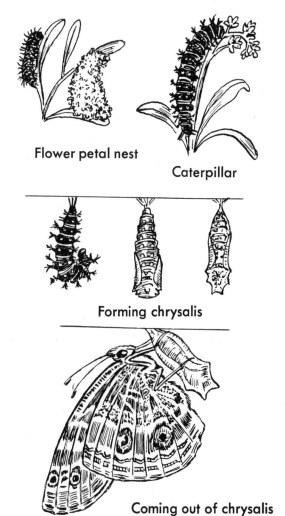

Flower petal nest

Caterpillar

Forming chrysalis

Coming out of chrysalis

PAINTED BEAUTY BUTTERFLY

Young

Full-grown

Caterpillars

Chrysalis

BLACK SWALLOWTAIL BUTTERFLY

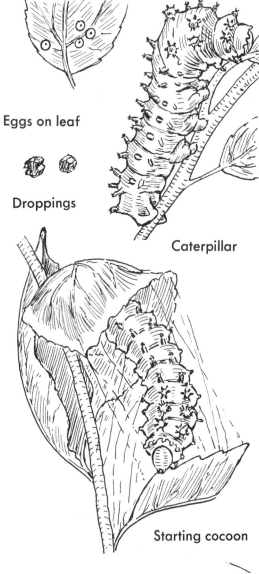

Eggs on leaf

Droppings

Caterpillar

Starting cocoon

MOTH CATERPILLARS

The large, fat caterpillars that are found on trees and bushes turn into giant moths. These caterpillars either form pupae inside cocoons or form uncovered pupae underground. The pupae live through the winter and change into moths the following spring.

CECROPIA

One of the largest and most common of these moths is the cecropia. Look for its caterpillar on wild cherry, willow, oak, apple, and other trees. The young caterpillar is first black, then orange, then yellow. After the fourth molt it has a green body that has blue, yellow, and orange knobs along the back and sides. When the caterpillar is 4 inches long, it is ready to make a cocoon. Holding onto a twig with its tail end, it swings its body back and forth while it spins silk from its mouth to make the cocoon. It also fastens the silk to the edge of leaves and pulls them together over the outside of the cocoon where they dry. The finished cocoon is fastened lengthwise to a twig.

You will find these cocoons in bushes and trees in fields and along roads. If you collect some, keep them in a cool place and moisten them once in a while. In June the moth will come out through a hole in the end of the cocoon.

The cecropia moth's wings are 5 or 6 inches across. They are brown and tan with red and white markings. The moth's body is rust-red with white lines and black spots. These moths do not eat. They live just long enough to mate and lay their eggs.

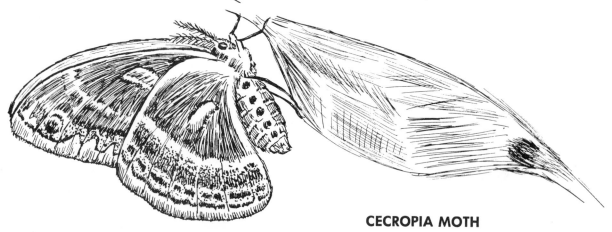

CECROPIA MOTH

ISABELLA TIGER MOTH

In fields and along roads in the fall you will find the black and brown woolly bear caterpillar. It is the larva of the Isabella tiger moth. Some people consider it a weather prophet; they say that if it is more brown than black there will be a mild winter.

In the fall these caterpillars are finished eating and are looking for a sheltered place to spend the winter. You can pick one up then to keep until spring. (It will curl up and play dead when you handle it.) Put it in a box that has air holes, and keep it in a cool place. In spring give it some grass, plantain, or clover to eat. About April, it will spin a hairy cocoon; at the end of May, the moth will come out of the cocoon.

The Isabella tiger moth is about 2 inches across. Its wings are yellowish-tan with dark specks, and its body is yellow with a row of dark spots down the back.

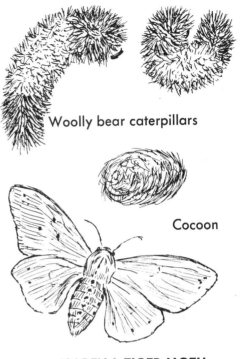

Woolly bear caterpillars

Cocoon

ISABELLA TIGER MOTH

TOMATO SPHINX MOTH

The large green or brown worm that you find on tomato vines may not make a handsome pet, but it is interesting to keep while it forms a pupa and changes into a moth.

Keep the worm in a container such as a gallon jar with netting over the top. Have a few inches of sand or earth in the bottom. Feed the worm fresh tomato leaves until it is full grown, about 4 inches long. A full-grown worm stops eating and begins to roam about. Soon it settles on the sand or earth at the bottom of the jar and begins to dig in. Instead of making a cocoon, it forms a hard-shelled pupa underground. The pupa is shaped like a jug; the handle encases the tongue of the developing moth. Leave the pupa in sand or earth in the jar through the winter. Keep it in a cool place and do not let it dry out. Late in spring the pupa will wriggle to the surface and change into a moth. Many tomato worms have parasites which destroy them before they have a chance to change.

The tomato sphinx moth is about 4½ inches across. Its wings are mottled gray and brown like the bark of a tree. Its body has a row of orange and black spots along each side. It has a very long tongue, curled up when not in use, with which it sips nectar from flowers.

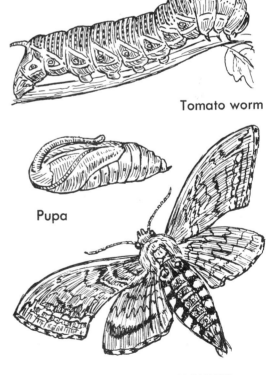

Tomato worm

Pupa

TOMATO SPHINX MOTH

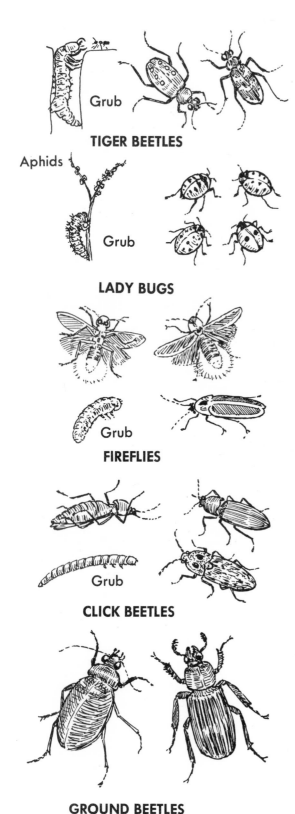

TIGER BEETLES

Aphids

Grub

LADY BUGS

Grub

FIREFLIES

Grub

CLICK BEETLES

GROUND BEETLES

BEETLES are fun to keep because of their bright colors and different ways of living and feeding.

Beetles lay eggs in the ground or on plants. The eggs hatch into grubs. These form pupae and change into beetles.

TIGER BEETLES have slender bodies and long legs on which they run after prey. One kind is bright blue-green with six white spots, another is purple with light markings. The grubs live in vertical holes in the ground. They stick their heads out of their holes and grab insects that come near. Keep beetles and grubs in a vivarium with moist sand on the bottom. Feed them small, soft-bodied, live insects.

LADY BUGS are a kind of beetle. Some of them are red or yellow with black spots; some are black with red or yellow spots. Some of the grubs are brightly colored. Lady bugs and grubs live on plants and eat aphids (tiny plant lice.) Keep an aphid-covered stem from a rose bush, daisy, or other plant in the vivarium with the lady bugs.

LIGHTENING BUGS or FIREFLIES are beetles. They are about ½ inch long. As they raise their dark wings when they fly, a bright light flashes from their tail end. You can catch fireflies in a jar at night.

The grubs of some kinds of fireflies are the glowworms that are found on the ground or in rotting wood. Keep a few fireflies and glowworms in a vivarium with sawdust or rotted wood, a growing plant, and some earth on the bottom. Some kinds of fireflies eat small insects; other kinds eat vegetable food including bananas.

CLICK BEETLES have slender dark bodies ½ inch long or longer. When placed on their backs, they can flip into the air and land right side up with the help of a flexible joint at the base of their wings. The grubs are called wireworms, and they live in the ground. Both beetles and grubs eat plant food such as rotted wood, roots, fruits, and boiled potato; they like a little water to drink.

GROUND BEETLES are black or brown, rather broad and flat, and about 1 inch long. They usually hide under logs or stones during the day and feed at night. Keep these beetles in a vivarium that has sawdust, some stones, and pieces of bark on the bottom. Feed them caterpillars, grubs, soft-bodied insects, and bits of raw meat.

SPIDERS are interesting to keep and watch. The kinds that are common in the northeastern part of the United States are not poisonous. Female spiders lay eggs in small silken cocoons or sacs. The eggs hatch into small spiders.

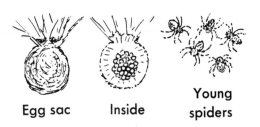

Egg sac   Inside   Young spiders

LIFE HISTORY

HOW TO KEEP AND FEED

Keep spiders in a vivarium that is big enough for them to move around in and make their webs. Put in a piece of sod, growing plants, or sticks to support the webs.

The spiders will eat live insects that you drop into their webs. Put in small insects like aphids, leaf hoppers, and flies for the smaller spiders; large insects like grasshoppers, crickets, and cockroaches for the larger spiders. Sprinkle the vivarium once in a while to furnish moisture.

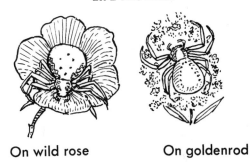

On wild rose   On goldenrod

CRAB SPIDERS

SPIDERS WITHOUT WEBS

The CRAB SPIDER has a large abdomen and stout front legs. It moves sideways and backwards like a crab. One kind, which grows to be ½ inch long, lives in flowers. In spring, when most flowers are pink or white, it has a white body with pink markings. Later, when it lives on goldenrod, its body is yellow. Keep this spider on a fresh flower. Put small insects on the flower for the spider to eat.

JUMPING SPIDERS are less than ½ inch long. Some kinds are brightly colored. These spiders catch their prey by leaping. Sometimes they jump long distances, spinning a thread of silk as they go. The male courts the female by dancing around her. Jumping spiders are found on plants or on buildings. Keep them in a dry, sunny place.

JUMPING SPIDERS

WOLF SPIDERS grow to be ½ to ¾ of an inch long. One kind is gray or brown and has yellow stripes down the back. The female lays her eggs in a sac, like a little football, that is attached to the spinnerets at the end of her body. After the young spiders hatch, they cling to the mother's abdomen for a while, giving her a fuzzy look.

These spiders catch their insect prey on the ground by stalking, and spring on it like a wolf. They lie in wait under stones or in holes that they dig in the ground and line with silk. Put a few inches of earth and some grass and stones in the bottom of their vivarium.

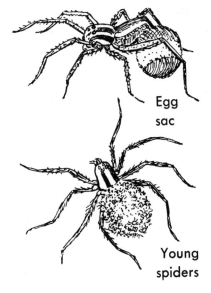

Egg sac

Young spiders

WOLF SPIDERS

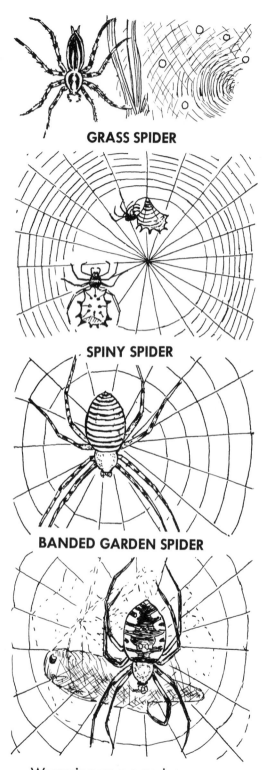

GRASS SPIDER

SPINY SPIDER

BANDED GARDEN SPIDER

Wrapping up a grasshopper

ORANGE GARDEN SPIDER

WEB-MAKING SPIDERS

GRASS SPIDERS make funnel-shaped webs on lawns and in fields. After a fog or heavy dew the webs glisten with drops of water. The spider hides in the center of the web until an insect falls in, then it dashes out to catch its prey. Grass spiders grow to be ⅜ to ¾ of an inch long. One kind is yellow or brown and has black lines on the back. Keep a grass spider in a container that has a piece of sod on the bottom. Feed it by dropping small insects into its web.

The SPINY SPIDER is often found in gardens. It grows to be about ¼ inch long and has a white abdomen with black, thorny points. The under part is black-and-white striped and comes to a point in the center where the spinnerets are. As the spider spins its finely woven, orb-shaped web, it guides the threads into place with one hind leg while it travels on the other legs. It may make a new web every morning. In the center of the web the spider waits for its prey. It stores dead insects on the outer threads.

The large, orb-shaped webs that are found in gardens and fields are made by the garden spiders. The BANDED GARDEN SPIDER has narrow black and yellow bands on its white abdomen, a white head, and yellow-and-black legs. The ORANGE GARDEN SPIDER has orange markings on its velvety black abdomen, a gray head, and orange and black legs. These are the female spiders; they grow to be about an inch long. The males are much smaller.

In autumn the females lay their eggs in an oval or a cup-shaped cocoon, or sac. The sac is fastened to a weed stalk or a leaf, and it hangs there through the winter. In spring the young spiders come out of the sac.

The web of a garden spider may be several feet across. Some spiders make a new web every day, some keep and repair the old one. The spider hides at the side of the web until an insect is caught. Then it rushes out and either eats the insect at once or wraps it in silk and leaves it dangling on the web. Drop a grasshopper into the spider's web and watch what happens.

Keep a garden spider in a large container such as a wood or cardboard box with a glass or plastic front and a screen over the top. Or leave the spider out of doors and watch it there. It usually stays in the same place.

PART III

SMALL MAMMALS
AND BIRDS

CAGES

A cage for a small animal is easily made from a box, a piece of glass, and wire mesh. The cage must be big enough to let the animal move freely.

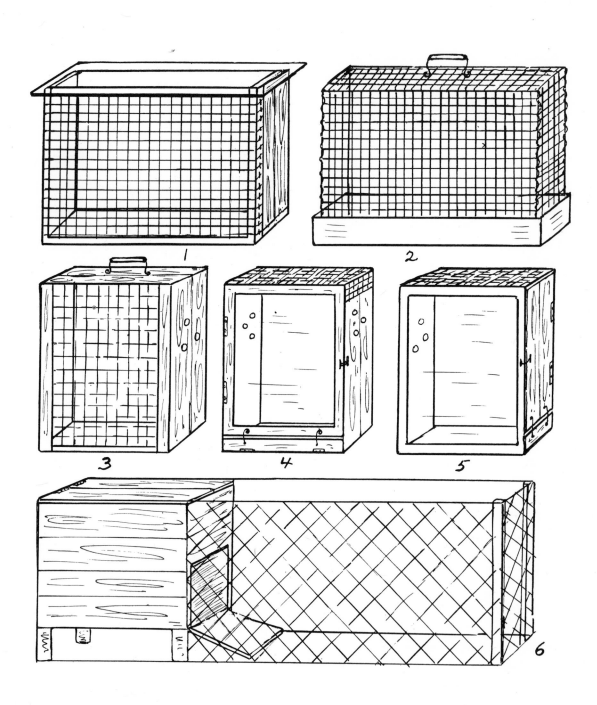

HOW TO MAKE

If an animal must be kept in a cage for a short time, be sure that the cage is airy and large enough for the animal to get some exercise.

The cages in the picture on the opposite page may be made at home. 1) A wooden box with the front removed. A piece of hardware cloth (wire mesh) is stretched across it and nailed at the sides. A removable piece of glass rests on top. 2) A cage made from a piece of wire mesh cut like the pattern on this page. The sides are bent down and bound with wire. A handle is fastened to the top, and the cage is set in a metal pan or tray. 3) A wooden box with a front screen door or with a wire mesh sliding door that goes up and down. 4) A wooden box with a wire mesh top and a glass door front. A hinged board under the door opens separately. 5) A wooden box with a wire mesh top, a glass window, and a side door with a hinged board under the door. 6) An outdoor home for larger animals. The nesting box has a roof that may be raised for cleaning; the lower front half of the box is cut out and slanted to the ground to make a ramp. To avoid dampness, the box is raised from the ground. A fence made of 1-inch mesh chicken wire encloses the yard; if necessary, the wire may enclose the top as well as the sides. The wire should go at least a foot underground so that animals cannot dig out.

If gnawing animals are kept in a wooden box, it may be necessary to cover the sides with wire mesh to prevent the animals from chewing their way out.

HOW TO FURNISH

A cage should be furnished to resemble an animal's natural home as much as possible. The floor may be covered with hay, straw, sawdust, wood shavings, sand, newspapers, paper towels, or shredded paper. Some kind of nesting box, shelf, or den should be included. Soft materials like pieces of old blanket may be used for nests.

Shallow, heavy dishes that cannot be tipped over should be used to hold moist food and water. Dry food like hay may be placed on a rack; dry grain and nut food on a shelf. For exercise, swings, see-saws, tree branches, or a wheel should be provided.

PATTERN FOR CAGE 2

Fruit basket

Cheese carton

Cigar box

Shelf

Shingles

Flat rocks

FOR NESTS AND DENS

Heavy dishes and rack

FOR FOOD AND WATER

Swing

Seesaw

Branch and wheel

FOR EXERCISE

MAMMALS

Mammals are animals — usually with fur — that nurse their young. Some baby mammals may be raised in cages; some older ones for a while.

MOUSE HOUSE

SQUIRREL QUARTERS

**Skunk, rabbit, and woodchuck in
OUTDOOR PEN**

HOW TO KEEP

Baby animals may not need to be confined in a cage, but they should be kept in a warm room, and they should have a nesting place such as a basket or box lined with soft material. If woodchucks, skunks, and cottontail rabbits are kept past the baby stage, they may be kept part of the time in an outdoor pen like the one at the bottom of page 58. Have a rack for food and a dish of water in the pen. A raccoon should have a tall, fenced enclosure with a tree or stump that it can climb.

Mice may be kept in a cage like 4 or 5 on page 58. Give them a nesting box or shelf, something to exercise on, and food and water containers. If you should have a sturdy doll's house with a glass front, use it for a cage.

Do not keep any kind of a squirrel in anything but a large cage with furniture for exercise.

To hold an animal while taking it out of its cage, put one hand underneath it for support and hold the loose skin at the back of its neck with your other hand. A very small animal may be held in one hand. Do not pick any animal up by the ears, neck, or tail.

HOW TO CLEAN CAGES

Wooden boxes are easier to clean if they are given two coats of waterproof varnish. For the floor, a metal tray that can be removed for cleaning is a help. A hinged board at the bottom of the cage is useful because it can be opened to slide the tray or other floor covering out without disturbing the rest of the cage. A sliding screen or door that can be raised from the floor serves the same purpose. In these cages the furniture should be fastened to the sides or to a shelf rather than to the floor. Soiled spots on the floor should be removed every day. Whatever is used for a floor covering should be kept dry and changed frequently.

About once a week the animals should be removed from the cage. Then the floor and walls should be given a thorough scrubbing with soap and water or a disinfectant like Lysol, Sodium Chlorofectant, or Pinuseptol. These products with directions for using them may be found at a drugstore. The cage should be thoroughly rinsed and dried before the animal is returned to it.

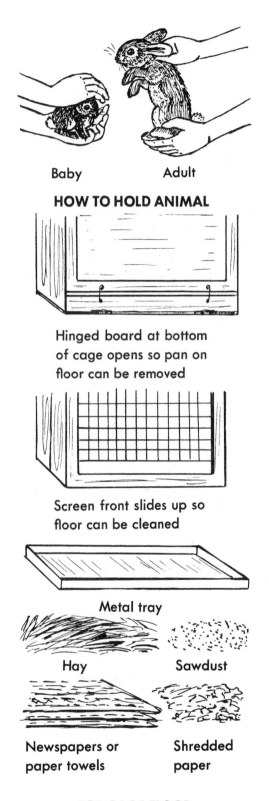

Baby   Adult

HOW TO HOLD ANIMAL

Hinged board at bottom of cage opens so pan on floor can be removed

Screen front slides up so floor can be cleaned

Metal tray

Hay   Sawdust

Newspapers or paper towels   Shredded paper

FOR CAGE FLOOR

The mother nurses the young

Feeding
by hand

Raccoons often
wash their food

HOW TO FEED

LIFE HISTORY

Mammals are animals that bear their young alive. The mothers nurse the young until they are able to feed themselves. Some of the young are without fur at first, but all of the animals in this section have fur when they are grown.

WHERE TO FIND

Small mammals are found in the woods and fields. Except in the case of mice, it is not good to set traps for them, and it is not kind to take them from their natural home if they are happy in it. Young orphan animals or injured older animals may be kept until they are strong enough to care for themselves. Half-wild pets that live out of doors but come to houses to be fed are often more interesting than pets that are confined in cages. In some states a permit is required to keep game animals.

HOW TO FEED

Feed animals the kind of food they are used to if it is possible. Give them as much as they want at one time once or twice a day. Put food in dishes on a shelf or in a rack. Do not put food on the ground where it may get soiled. A dish of fresh water should be available all the time. Gnawing animals need sticks or old bones to chew on.

KINDS OF FOOD

MEAT FOOD includes: raw lean beef, beef bones, liver; raw fish; beetles, grasshoppers, crickets, cockroaches, and other insects and their grubs; earthworms; eggs, cheese, and milk.

GRAIN and NUT FOOD includes: corn, oats, whole wheat, bread crusts, and crumbled dog biscuit; seeds from weeds, millet, sunflowers, cones of evergreen trees, or birdseed mixtures; acorns; hickory, beech, and hazelnuts, and butternuts; *not* peanuts.

VEGETABLE and FRUIT FOOD includes: lettuce, cabbage, spinach, carrots, beets and their tops, celery tops, green beans, peas on the vine, sweet potatoes, clover; mushrooms and tree buds for squirrels; apples, bananas and berries.

BABY ANIMALS

Baby animals that have lost their mothers may be raised in captivity until they are old enough to take care of themselves. Nursing animals may be fed milk from a small bottle with a fine nipple such as a doll's bottle, or from a medicine dropper. The milk may be canned evaporated milk diluted with an equal amount of water, or fresh cow's milk, plain or with a little Karo syrup added. A few drops of cod-liver oil may be added occasionally. The milk should be warmed and given about every two hours during the day with one late feeding at bedtime. When the baby animal grows teeth and shows an interest in solid food, it may be given pablum cereal powder or whole wheat bread crumbs in warm milk at first, and later regular food.

WOODCHUCKS are born in an underground burrow in spring, two to six in a family. Their eyes open at four weeks and at about six weeks they are ready for solid food. Woodchucks eat vegetables and fruits. They feed in the early morning and evening.

SKUNKS, four to eight in a family, are born in spring in a burrow, a hollow log, a cave, or sometimes under a house. They open their eyes at three weeks and are ready for solid food at about two months. Skunks eat meat and vegetable foods. A pet skunk should be taken to a veterinarian to have its scent glands removed when it is about a month old.

COTTONTAIL RABBITS have several families a year with four to seven in a family. Their home is a hollow in the ground, usually under weeds or other plants. The mother rabbit covers the young with a blanket of grass and fur, and leaves them during the day. She nurses them at night. If the nest is disturbed, the mother may not return to it. Baby rabbits open their eyes and ears in about a week and in two weeks they are ready for solid food.

Rabbits do most of their eating at night. Pets may be fed grain food in the morning and vegetable food at night.

Baby RACCOONS are born in spring, two to six in a family. They live in a hollow log, a cave, or other shelter. At three weeks they open their eyes; at two months they hunt for their own food. Young pet raccoons that are ready for solid food will eat meat, vegetable, and fruit foods. Give them water, since they like to wash their food.

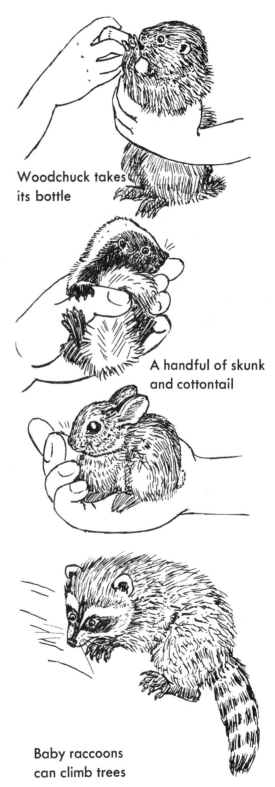

Woodchuck takes its bottle

A handful of skunk and cottontail

Baby raccoons can climb trees

BABY ANIMALS

BABY FLYING SQUIRREL

Taking milk from
medicine dropper

BABY GRAY SQUIRREL

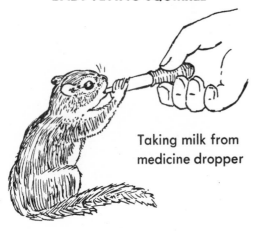

RED SQUIRREL

CHIPMUNK

SQUIRRELS

Squirrels make good outdoor pets. If food is set out for them, they will usually come near houses. They like grain, nuts, vegetables, and a little meat, and water to drink. Baby squirrels may be given milk from a small bottle or a medicine dropper until they have teeth. Then they may be given whole wheat bread soaked in milk; baby cereal; raw or partly cooked eggs; and vegetables.

Squirrels are very active. If they must be kept in a cage, it should be a large one containing swings, bars, a tree branch, or an exercise wheel. They have sharp teeth and can gnaw their way out of any but a stout cage.

FLYING SQUIRRELS live in the woods and are active at night. They are able to flatten out and glide from one tree to another. In spring two to six young are born in a hole in a tree. At four weeks they open their eyes; at two months they can climb trees and make short glides. The family stays together most of the year. Flying squirrels make gentle and playful pets that may be kept in a room or a screened porch. They scamper at night and sleep in the daytime.

GRAY SQUIRRELS live near houses and in parks as well as in the woods. They have two families of from one to six young in a season. The young open their eyes after five weeks and come out of the nest a week later. They stay with the mother until they are nearly grown. Gray squirrels become tame, but they may bite or scratch if handled. Be careful if you pick up an injured squirrel.

RED SQUIRRELS live in woods, especially woods that have evergreen trees. They are more aggressive than gray squirrels and will drive them away. Young squirrels are born in a nest in a hollow tree. There are three to six in a family, and there may be two families a season. The young open their eyes after four weeks and are weaned after five weeks. The family stays together through the summer. Adult red squirrels do not tame easily, but the babies may be kept until they are nearly grown.

CHIPMUNKS live in stone walls, under logs, or in underground burrows. Four to six young are born in spring and another family may be born in fall. The young open their eyes after one month and at three months they have teeth. They stay with the mother through summer.

MICE

Wild mice make pretty and interesting pets. Their cage, or mouse house, may be furnished with small articles, such as tiny ladders, see-saws, and dolls' furniture, or with a tree branch and nesting boxes. A pair of mice may be kept together, but the male should be removed if there are babies. Two males in a cage may fight.

Mice will eat: grain food including wild seeds and bird-seed; some small nuts; vegetables and fruits including wild berries and rose hips. Meat food, including cheese, is not good for pet mice because it may give them a tendency to eat each other. Mice should be fed morning and night.

The WHITE-FOOTED OR DEER MOUSE lives in the woods. In fall and winter it sometimes gets into country houses. This mouse has a grayish-brown back and is white underneath. It keeps its fur neat, but not its nest. When one nest is soiled, it moves to a new one. Several families of from one to nine young mice are born in a season. The young open their eyes soon after two weeks and may breed when a little over a month old.

The MEADOW MOUSE OR VOLE is stout-bodied and short-tailed. It lives in an underground tunnel or in the grass in fields or light woods. Many families of from four to eight young mice are born during a year. The young have their eyes and ears open and have a coat of fur after eight or nine days. When about a month old they are able to breed.

Some kinds of JUMPING MICE live in dry places, other kinds live in moist woods. These mice have long hind legs and long tails. They are able to jump a distance of several feet. In winter they hibernate in underground burrows; in summer they live in grass and weeds in a rounded nest made of grass and leaves. In spring a family of two to six young is born. The young are full grown at six weeks. Jumping mice make tame but nervous pets. They should be kept in a large cage.

The HARVEST MOUSE is a little smaller and more slender than the common house mouse. It has a longer tail and is a cleaner creature. It is found in the warmer parts of the United States in fields and marshes. It makes a rounded, grass nest lined with plant down. In spring and fall these mice have families of from two to six young. The young care for themselves when three or four weeks old.

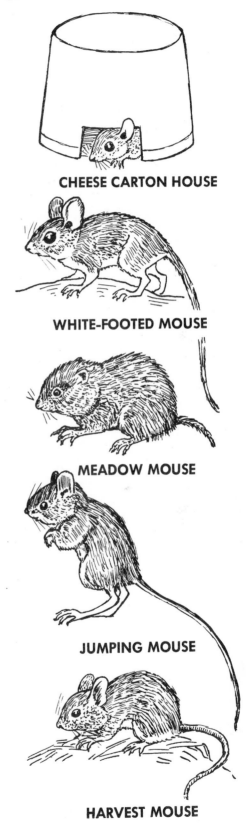

CHEESE CARTON HOUSE

WHITE-FOOTED MOUSE

MEADOW MOUSE

JUMPING MOUSE

HARVEST MOUSE

BIRDS

Young or injured birds may be kept in cages, but healthy adult birds should be watched outdoors. Birdhouses and feeding stations bring them near.

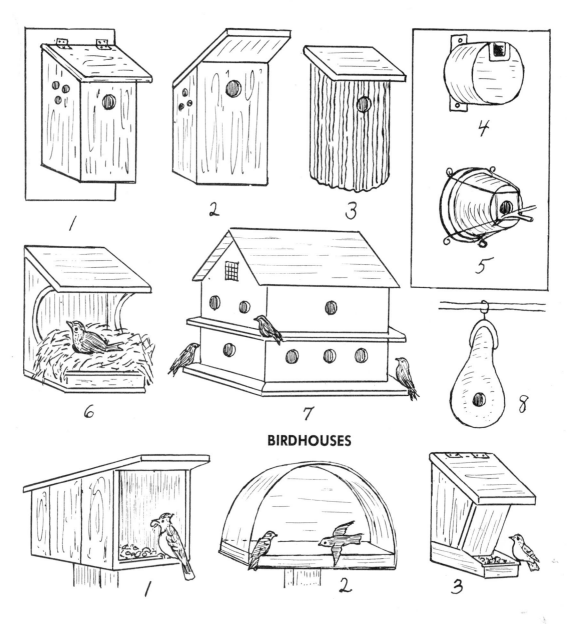

BIRDHOUSES

FEEDING STATIONS

HOW TO ATTRACT

A wild bird should not be kept in a cage unless it has been injured or left an orphan. If you have a bird bath or pool, a feeding station, and birdhouses, birds will come to feed and raise their families where you can watch them out of doors.

A birdhouse that is to be used for more than one year should have either a roof, a floor, or a door that can be opened for cleaning. The entrance hole should be near the top and the right size for the bird that you wish to attract: 1 inch for wrens, 1⅛ for chickadees, 1½ for bluebirds, 2 inches for flycatchers, 2½ for martins, etc. Rough bark or grooves inside the house below the hole will give the baby birds a ladder to climb up.

The houses pictured on page 66 can be made or bought. 1) and 2) Wooden box-type houses. 3) A piece of hollow log with a roof. 4) A tin can with a hole that is bound with tape. 5) A flower pot with the hole enlarged. 6) A roofed shelf. 7) An apartment house for martins. 8) A hollow gourd.

Covered feeding stations for winter should face away from the strongest winds. 1) A wooden box with an open front. 2) A platform with a roof made of a curved wooden frame covered with strong plastic material. 3) A wooden container, with a hinged roof, that is filled with birdseed which flows into a bottom tray.

A bird bath may be made from any kind of a shallow container placed on a post, stump, or rock. A small pool may be made by lining a hollow in the ground with cement.

HOW TO KEEP

To keep a bird for a short time, a cage like 2 or 3 on page 58 may be used. The cage should be furnished with branches, bars, or swings for exercise, and dishes for food, drink, and bathing. The floor should be covered with a tray containing sand or fine gravel. If a tray is not handy, put newspapers or paper towels on the floor. The floor should be cleaned every day. In the box cage in the picture, the wire mesh front slides up so that the floor can be cleaned without removing the bird. The wire cage pictured may be lifted off the pan that it rests in.

BIRD BATH and POOL

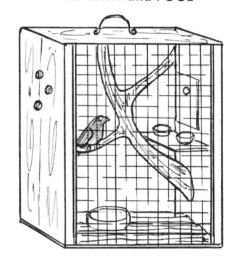

Box cage—wire mesh doors slide up and down

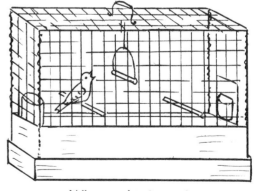

Wire or plastic mesh cage set in large pan

BIRD CAGES

Egg and newly-hatched young in nest

LIFE HISTORY

Suet tied
to tree

In net bag

In holes in stick

Grain on ground

HOW TO FEED

LIFE HISTORY

Birds lay eggs, usually in nests, in trees or bushes, on the ground, in banks or cliffs, in or on buildings. The eggs of songbirds hatch into helpless baby birds which are blind and without feathers. The parents bring food to them until they are able to leave the nest, and sometimes long afterward.

WHERE TO FIND

Birds are everywhere out of doors, and that is the best place for them unless they cannot care for themselves.

HOW TO FEED

Birds that have short broad beaks are usually seed and nut eaters. Birds with narrow, pointed beaks are insect eaters. Here is a list of bird food that you can put outside or feed to captive adult birds.

For seed and nut eaters: rolled oats, cracked corn, popcorn, hominy, boiled rice, rye, barley, wheat and buckwheat; dry bread crumbs; peanuts and peanut butter; sunflower and apple seeds; dried squash, pumpkin, and melon seeds; weed, grass, and millet seeds; baby chick scratch feed from a feed store and birdseed from a store; acorns and cracked nuts; cones; grapes, berries, and raisins soaked in water; lettuce, clover, water cress, and chickweed.

For insect eaters: live insects, earthworms, meal worms (from a pet store), caterpillars and spiders; bits of raw meat, cracked meat bones and fish bones; cottage cheese and chopped hard-boiled egg. A good winter food is a piece of suet fastened to a tree. It may be tied on with a string or hung in a net bag. A crocheted bag or a cut-down net orange or potato bag is good. A wire container is bad for the birds' feet in freezing weather. The suet (fat) may also be melted and poured into holes that have been bored in a stick.

Birds need grit to help digest their food. Most birdseed and chick feed mixtures that you buy contain grit. Sand or ashes put out with bird food in winter will furnish grit.

A container of water should be near the bird food.

BABY SONGBIRDS

Baby songbirds are fed and cared for by their parents. If you find baby birds, either in a nest or on the ground, that have parents to look after them, do not disturb them. But if you should find a little bird that you know has lost its parents, you might take it and raise it until it is big enough to fly and take care of itself. In all states it is against the law to have captive songbirds.

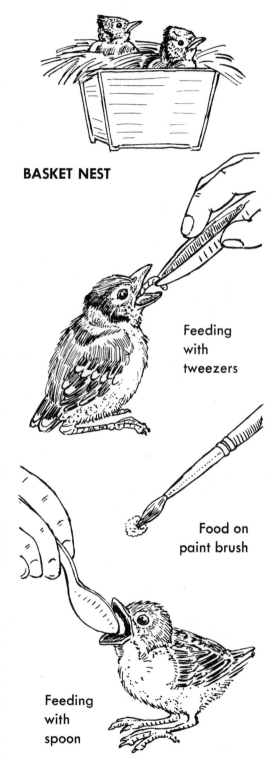

BASKET NEST

HOW TO KEEP

Make a soft nest for the baby bird by lining a box or basket with a wool cloth, cotton batting, dry grass, or hay. Keep it in a warm place where it will get some sun. If the bird is very active, the nest may be kept inside a cage.

Feeding
with
tweezers

HOW TO FEED

Parent birds feed young ones often. If you raise a baby bird, you will have to feed it often, too—every half hour or oftener for the first two weeks, then about every hour until it is able to feed itself. Drop the food down its throat with your fingers, with tweezers or forceps, or with a spoon or small paint brush. If the bird doesn't open its beak voluntarily, you can pry it open gently from each side. Be sure that the bird has swallowed one mouthful before giving it another.

Food on
paint brush

While the little bird is being fed soft food, it will not need water. When it is able to feed itself, it should have a dish of fresh water handy all the time. If the bird doesn't know how to drink, you can teach it. Drop a little water down its throat with a medicine dropper, then dip its bill into the water dish.

Baby birds will eat: baby chick feed (growing mash moistened with water); grated hard-boiled egg alone, or mixed with a few drops of cod-liver oil and cracker crumbs dipped in milk; whole wheat bread crumbs soaked in milk; a little raw chopped beef; chopped earthworms; small soft-bodied insects.

Feeding
with
spoon

Birds that eat seeds when they are grown, eat insects and other soft food when they are babies. As soon as they can feed themselves, they will eat the same food as adults.

HOW TO FEED

ROBINS nest near houses

BLUE JAYS come for peanuts

CROWS collect things

Baby SCREECH OWL   Baby BARN OWL

TAME BIRDS OUTDOORS AND IN

Outdoor birds that become tame are fun to watch.

ROBINS live near houses. They build their nests on low branches of trees or in bushes. You can watch them collect leaves, twigs, grass, and mud for their nests. You can see how the mother bird rounds out the inside by sitting in the nest and turning around. Later you will see four or five greenish-blue eggs. After about two weeks, baby birds hatch. The parents feed them constantly for about two weeks until they are able to fly. Even when they are big enough to feed themselves, the young ones follow the parents around begging for food.

BLUE JAYS also live near houses. They defend their nests vigorously. If you come near, they are likely to swoop down and try to chase you away. After the young ones grow up, the whole family will come to a feeding station. They will eat almost anything, but are especially fond of peanuts. Sometimes a jay will stuff a peanut down its throat and take another in its bill. Then it may store the peanuts in a tree or under leaves. Sometimes it watches a squirrel bury a nut and digs it up after the squirrel leaves.

CROWS that are cared for while young become tame. They make interesting and intelligent, but mischievous pets. They can imitate sounds and almost talk to you. They collect shiny objects like coins and silver spoons and hide them. They also steal eggs and young birds from songbirds' nests, since they are meat-eaters as well as grain-eaters. Crows have big appetites. A pet crow may be fed worms, insects, mice, dog ration, corn, fruit, bread soaked in milk, meat, and bones. There is no law against keeping a pet crow.

SCREECH and BARN OWLS become tame if cared for while young. The young of these two owls are light colored and fluffy. The screech owl has small ear tufts; the barn owl has a heart-shaped, monkey-like face. Although owls are active at night, pets learn to eat in the daytime. Every hour or two feed baby owls earthworms or milk from a medicine dropper. Older owls will eat raw beef, liver, fish, chicken heads, and meat bones. They spit out a pellet containing the parts they can't digest. When the owls are grown, they should be set free to hunt their own food. They help farmers by catching many insects and mice.

INDEX

MORE TO READ

AMPHIBIANS

Book of Reptiles and Amphibians, The, by Michael Bevans (Garden City)

Bufo, The Story of a Toad, by Robert McClung (Morrow)

Field Guide to Reptiles and Amphibians, by Roger Conant (Houghton)

Reptiles and Amphibians, by Herbert S. Zim and Hobart M. Smith (Simon and Schuster)

Tree Frog, by Paul McCutcheon Sears (Holiday)

BIRDS

Birds in the Garden, by Margaret McKenney (Grosset)

Birds in Your Backyard, by Ted Pettit (Harper)

How To Watch Birds, by Roger Barton (McGraw Hill)

INSECTS AND SPIDERS

Crickets, by Olive L. Earle (Morrow)

Field Guide to the Butterflies, A, by Alexander B. Klots (Houghton)

Firefly, by Paul McCutcheon Sears (Holiday)

Grasshopper Book, by Wilfrid Bronson (Harcourt)

Insects, by Herbert S. Zim & Clarence Cottam (Simon & Schuster)

Insects and the Homes They Build, by Dorothy Sterling (Doubleday)

Insects and Their Ways, by Bertha Morris Parker (Row, Peterson)

Junior Book of Insects, by Edwin Way Teale (Dutton)

Monarch Butterfly, by Marion W. Marcher (Holiday)

Spider Book, by John Henry Comstock (Comstock)

Wonder World of Ants, The, by Wilfrid Bronson (Harcourt)

MAMMALS

Field Guide to the Mammals, A, by William Burt and Richard Grossenheider (Houghton)

Mammals of North America, by Victor H. Cahalane (Macmillan)

Mammals, by Herbert S. Zim and Donald F. Hoffmeister (Simon and Schuster)

PETS

Animal Inn, by Virginia Moe (Houghton Mifflin)

Book of Wild Pets, The, by Clifford B. Moore (Branford)

Enjoying Pets, by J. Bentley Aistrop (Vanguard)

Homemade Zoo, by Sylvia Greenberg and Edith Raskin (McKay)

How To Make a Miniature Zoo, by Vinson Brown (Little Brown)

Odd Pets, by Dorothy Childs Hogner (Crowell)

Pets, by Frances N. Crystie (Little Brown)

PLANTS

Field Book of American Trees and Shrubs, by F. Schuyler Mathews (Putnam)

Field Book of American Wild Flowers, by F. Schuyler Mathews (Putnam)

Field Guide to the Ferns, A, by Boughton Cobb (Houghton Mifflin)

Wild Flower Guide, by Edgar T. Wherry (Doubleday)

REPTILES

Book of Reptiles and Amphibians, The, by Michael Bevans (Garden City)

Field Guide to Reptiles and Amphibians, A, by Roger Conant (Houghton)

Reptiles and Amphibians, by Herbert S. Zim and Hobart M. Smith (Simon and Schuster)

Horned Lizards, by DeVault and Munch (Steck)

All About Snakes, by Bessie M. Hect (Random)

Boy's Book of Snakes, by Percy A. Morris (Ronald)

Field Book of Snakes of the United States and Canada, by Karl P. Schmidt and D. Dwight Davis (Putnam)

Field Book of Snakes, by Zim (Morrow)

Slim Green (Story of a snake), by Harris & Dyer (Little Brown)

Handbook of Turtles, by Archie Carr (Cornell)

Turtles of the United States and Canada, by Clifford Pope (Knopf)

Turtles, by Wilfrid Bronson (Harcourt)

GENERAL

Exploring Nature with Your Child, by Dorothy Edwards Shuttlesworth (Greystone)

Fieldbook of Natural History, by E. Laurence Palmer (McGraw Hill)

Field Book of Nature Activities, by William Hillcourt (Putnam)

Hammond's Guide to Nature Hobbies, by E. L. Jordan (Hammond)

In Woods and Fields, by Margaret Waring Buck (Abingdon)

Nature Notebook, by Robert Candy (Houghton Mifflin)

MAGAZINES

Audubon Magazine, published by National Audubon Society, New York City

Junior Natural History, published by American Museum of Natural History, New York City

National Geographic Magazine, published by National Geographic Society, Washington, D. C.

Natural History, published by American Museum of Natural History, New York City

Nature Magazine, published by American Nature Association, Washington, D. C.

BULLETINS AND LEAFLETS

Audubon Nature Bulletins, published by the National Audubon Society, 1130 Fifth Avenue, New York 28, New York

Turtox Service Leaflets, published by General Biological Supply House, 761-763 East 69th Place, Chicago 37, Illinois

To learn more about animals in the wild and as pets, join the Junior or Senior Audubon Society.